Overcoming Alcohol Problems

Overcoming Alcohol Problems

Workbook for Couples

Barbara S. McCrady • Elizabeth E. Epstein

OXFORD
UNIVERSITY PRESS

2009

OXFORD
UNIVERSITY PRESS

Oxford University Press, Inc., publishes works that further
Oxford University's objective of excellence
in research, scholarship, and education.

Oxford   New York
Auckland   Cape Town   Dar es Salaam   Hong Kong   Karachi
Kuala Lumpur   Madrid   Melbourne   Mexico City   Nairobi
New Delhi   Shanghai   Taipei   Toronto

With offices in
Argentina   Austria   Brazil   Chile   Czech Republic   France   Greece
Guatemala   Hungary   Italy   Japan   Poland   Portugal   Singapore
South Korea   Switzerland   Thailand   Turkey   Ukraine   Vietnam

Published by Oxford University Press, Inc.
198 Madison Avenue, New York, New York 10016

www.oup.com

Oxford is a registered trademark of Oxford University Press

ISBN 978-0-19-532275-0

About Treatments*ThatWork*™

One of the most difficult problems confronting patients with various disorders and diseases is finding the best help available. Everyone is aware of friends or family who have sought treatment from a seemingly reputable practitioner, only to find out later from another doctor that the original diagnosis was wrong or the treatments recommended were inappropriate or perhaps even harmful. Most patients, or family members, address this problem by reading everything they can about their symptoms, seeking out information on the Internet, or aggressively "asking around" to tap knowledge from friends and acquaintances. Governments and healthcare policymakers are also aware that people in need do not always get the best treatments—something they refer to as "variability in healthcare practices."

Now healthcare systems around the world are attempting to correct this variability by introducing "evidence-based practice." This simply means that it is in everyone's interest that patients get the most up-to-date and effective care for a particular problem. Healthcare policymakers have also recognized that it is very useful to give consumers of healthcare as much information as possible, so that they can make intelligent decisions in a collaborative effort to improve physical health and mental health. This series, Treatments*ThatWork*™, is designed to accomplish just that. Only the latest and most effective interventions for particular problems are described in user-friendly language. To be included in this series, each treatment program must pass the highest standards of evidence available, as determined by a scientific advisory board. Thus, when individuals suffering from these problems or their family members seek out an expert clinician who is familiar with these interventions and decides that they are appropriate, they will have confidence that they are receiving the best care available. Of course, only your health care professional can decide on the right mix of treatments for you.

This workbook describes a scientifically based and proven effective treatment for alcohol problems. It is designed to be used by couples who are attending sessions with a qualified mental health professional because one partner is experiencing problems with alcohol.

If you or your partner is dealing with an alcohol problem, the program outlined in this book can help you both. Over the course of 12 sessions with a therapist, the drinking partner will be taught various skills and strategies for quitting drinking, as well as dealing with high-risk situations in which there is a strong temptation to drink. Throughout the program, the non-drinking partner will learn how to provide support and change certain behaviors that may contribute to the drinking partner's problem. As a couple, you will practice communication skills and participate in pleasant activities in order to improve your relationship and enhance intimacy. You and your partner will work together to overcome the drinking problem once and for all.

Teamwork and dedication are required for a successful outcome. If you and your partner are motivated and willing to work together, you will no doubt find yourselves on the way to a healthier and happier relationship at the end of treatment.

David H. Barlow, Editor-in-Chief,
Treatments *That Work*™
Boston, MA

Contents

Chapter 1   Session 1: Introduction / Rationale / Self-Recording   *1*

Chapter 2   Session 2: Functional Analysis / Noticing Positive Behavior   *25*

Chapter 3   Session 3: High-Risk Hierarchy / Partner Functional Analysis Part I / Self-Management Plans   *41*

Chapter 4   Session 4: Partner Functional Analysis Part II / Enhancing Motivation to Change   *57*

Chapter 5   Session 5: Dealing with Urges / Decreasing Partner Triggers   *69*

Chapter 6   Session 6: Rearranging Behavioral Consequences / Shared Activities   *83*

Chapter 7   Session 7: Dealing With Alcohol-Related Thoughts / Communication Part I   *97*

Chapter 8   Session 8: Drink Refusal / Communication Part II   *109*

Chapter 9   Session 9: Partner Role in Drink Refusal / Communication Part III / Relapse Prevention Part I   *117*

Chapter 10   Session 10: Problem Solving / Relapse Prevention Part II   *129*

Chapter 11   Session 11: Relapse Prevention Part III / Acceptance Framework   *145*

Chapter 12   Session 12: Review / Relapse Prevention Part IV   *157*

Appendix of Forms   *163*

Client Self-Monitoring Cards   *169*

Partner Recording Cards   *199*

Chapter 1

Session 1: Introduction / Rationale / Self-Recording

Goals

- To learn about this program and what it will involve

- For you and your partner to commit to the program and sign a treatment contract

- To review the results of your pretreatment assessment

- To begin self-monitoring

- To talk about ways of achieving abstinence and develop an abstinence plan

- To plan how to deal with any upcoming high-risk situations in which you may be tempted to drink

The Journey Begins

Together in this therapy, we are starting a journey. The most successful and ambitious journeys all start with a road map (a plan) and a destination (a goal). The goals are sobriety and a happier relationship. The road map is this therapy. You will learn ways of quitting drinking and improving your life.

You will work together with your partner and therapist to identify high-risk situations that may lead to drinking. Some of these situations will involve places, people, and things that you come across. Some of these situations will involve thoughts and emotions that are connected to your use. Some of these situations may come from your relationships. Your therapist will help you develop a plan and the skills to get through these tough situations. In each session, you will be introduced to a new skill or technique for dealing with high-risk situations.

The road will get bumpy at times. Sometimes things may be so rough that you will wonder if you've made a wrong turn. Many people who decide to quit drinking have a tough time in the beginning. Some people get discouraged by the tough times. Other people see these challenging times as a chance to learn more about themselves. Whatever happens, look at these tough times as chances to learn more about what kinds of situations are risky and what it takes to get through them.

When learning to ride a bicycle, most people will fall a few times. Most everyone gets back on the bicycle and eventually succeeds in learning to ride. You may go down the wrong path during this journey. If you do, recognizing this will be important so you can get back on the right road.

One very important part of this therapy is your commitment to working with your therapist. Each week you will be asked to do things outside of sessions. It is very important that you work hard at home. Work outside sessions is as important as work during sessions.

Many individuals have succeeded with this program. The things taught in this program help people stop drinking and build better relationships.

The Plan

Over the course of this program you will:

1. Study your drinking habits. Figure out what leads to drinking and what keeps it going.

2. Change habits and things around you that lead to or encourage drinking.

3. Learn positive alternatives to drinking alcohol.

Your therapist will help you through these steps during the next 12 weeks. In the first three sessions, the focus will be on step one. As part of step one, you will look at what people, places, and things lead to drinking. You will also look at what happens because of drinking.

The following is a list of some important points about the treatment program you are about to begin.

- People with problems similar to yours have learned to stop drinking.

- Drinking is something you have learned to do. Habits can be changed. Right now, it does not matter how the drinking got started; it is important to figure out how to change.

- The goal is to be totally abstinent—to stop drinking altogether. Drinking should stop early on in the treatment. Sometimes people will have slips, but successful people learn from mistakes and get back with the program.

- Work in between sessions is as important as work during sessions. There will be things that you will be asked to do to learn and practice new skills. Practice is the only way to get this right. Often it is not possible to learn everything well during the session. If you do not complete the tasks required, your therapist reserves the right to reschedule your session in order to give you an opportunity to make up the work.

For the Partner

This treatment addresses both alcohol problems and relationship difficulties. Including a spouse or partner in alcohol treatment can improve the chances for the drinker to be successful in quitting drinking. Another reason you have been asked to participate in this program is because problem drinking can create pressures that threaten the health of a relationship.

As you may notice from the introduction to therapy, much of this treatment will focus on helping your partner quit drinking. Especially at first, the treatment will concentrate on understanding and fixing the problem drinking. As therapy continues, more attention will be placed on improving the way you get along with each other.

It is expected that your happiness with your relationship will increase as the drinking stops. Also, you and your partner will be introduced to many techniques that have helped other couples become happier. All couples can benefit from this special attention, no matter how happy they are when they begin therapy. You and your partner will both benefit from this experience. Imagine what life will be like without drinking and relationship problems!

Before treatment starts, please review the following list of rules and guidelines that you will be expected to follow.

1. Come to all the sessions with your partner. This treatment involves both of you.

2. Work on the assignments between sessions. What you see and experience during the week will help the treatment be successful. You will be asked to

observe and practice many things that will help both you and your partner.

3. Be patient! Both the drinking and any trouble in your relationship come from a long history of habits that have become well practiced over time. Both you and your partner will need to work hard and long to change these habits. Big change will not happen overnight, but will come with dedication to success.

4. Believe in yourself and your partner.

5. If you would like help with other problems of your own, speak to your therapist and he or she will guide you to the right kind of help.

It is important that both you and your partner commit to this program and agree to complete the tasks that are required of you in order to get the most benefit from treatment. Please read and sign the following brief treatment contract.

1. I understand that this treatment will include 12 sessions over 3 months and I agree to participate for that length of time. If I want to withdraw from the program, I agree to discuss this decision with my therapist prior to taking this action.

2. I agree to attend all sessions and to be prompt. If it is absolutely necessary that I cancel a session, I will call in advance to reschedule. I also agree to call in advance if I will be late to a session.

3. (Drinker Only) I understand that this treatment is intended for people who want to abstain from alcohol. I understand that I must work on remaining clean and sober.

4. I agree that it is essential for me to come to the session alcohol-free. I understand that I will be asked to leave any session to which I come with a blood alcohol level of over .05. I will be required to arrange safe transportation home.

5. I understand that I will be given a breath test for alcohol use each session.

6. I understand that I will be expected to practice some of the skills I discuss in treatment. I agree to bring in the workbook with the completed homework each week to discuss with my therapist.

7. I will be expected to attend all scheduled weekly sessions as research has shown that this type of treatment is effective only if both partners attend scheduled appointments on a regular basis.

I have reviewed the above statements with my therapist and I agree to abide by them.

_____   _____
Client   Date

_____   _____
Partner   Date

_____   _____
Therapist   Date

Prior to starting treatment, you and your partner completed an intake assessment where you filled out self-reports and questionnaires. These measures help your therapist better understand your drinking problem and they provide vital information your therapist can use to tailor the treatment program to fit your needs. You may have also been advised to visit your physician for a medical check-up. Since alcohol is a toxin and heavy drinking can affect your liver and other vital organs, it is a good idea to see your general practitioner to assess your health. Ask your doctor to perform the following tests and bring the lab results in to share with your therapist.

- Gamma glutamic transpeptidase (GGTP)

- Aspartate aminotransferase (AST)

- Alanine aminotransferase (ALT)

- Mean corpuscular volume (MCV)

- Bilirubin

- Uric acid

After covering the introductory material in the first session, your therapist will review with you and your partner the results of the pretreatment assessment. He or she will work with you to complete Feedback Sheets. Your therapist may provide you with data and have you fill out the sheets on your own. Blank sheets for your use are provided on pages 11–13. Alternatively, your therapist may complete the sheets for you.

Alcohol Information

Before reviewing the results of your assessment with your therapist, you should familiarize yourself with Tables 1.1–1.4, which provide information about alcohol and alcohol use. Your therapist will review this information with you in session.

Table 1.1 Alcohol Information

Beer	Standard drinks			
Ounces	Light	Regular	European	Ice
12	.75	1	1.25	1.5
16	1	1.33	1.66	—

Wine 5 ounces = 1 standard drink

Amount	Ounces	Standard drinks
750 ml	25.6	5
1.5 L	51	10

Hard Liquor
1.5 ounces of 80 proof liquor = 1 standard drink

Liquor			Equivalent number of standard drinks		
Amount	Street name	Ounces	80 proof	100 proof	190 proof
	"Shot"	1.5	1	1.25	2.38
200 ml	"Half pint"	6.8	4.5	5.67	10.77
375 ml	"Pint"	12.75	8.5	10.63	20.19
750 m	"Fifth"	25.5	17	21.25	40.38
1.75 L	"Half Gallon"	59.5	40	49.58	94.21

Table 1.2 Blood Alcohol Level Estimation Charts

Men									
Approximate Blood Alcohol Percentage									
Drinks	Body Weight in Pounds								Sample Behavioral Effects
	100	120	140	160	180	200	220	240	
0	.00	.00	.00	.00	.00	.00	.00	.00	Only completely safe limit
1	.04	.03	.03	.02	.02	.02	.02	.02	Impairment begins
2	.08	.06	.05	.05	.04	.04	.03	.03	Driving skills significantly affected; Information processing altered
3	.11	.09	.08	.07	.06	.06	.05	.05	
4	.15	.12	.11	.09	.08	.08	.07	.06	
5	.19	.16	.13	.12	.11	.09	.09	.08	
6	.23	.19	.16	.14	.13	.11	.10	.09	Legally intoxicated; Criminal penalties; Reaction time slowed; Loss of balance; Impaired movement; Slurred speech
7	.26	.22	.19	.16	.15	.13	.12	.11	
8	.30	.25	.21	.19	.17	.15	.14	.13	
9	.34	.28	.24	.21	.19	.17	.15	.14	
10	.38	.31	.27	.23	.21	.19	.17	.16	
One drink is 1.5 oz. shot of hard liquor, 12 oz. of beer, or 5 oz. of table wine.									

continued

Table 1.2 Blood Alcohol Level Estimation Charts *continued*

Women										
Approximate Blood Alcohol Percentage										
Drinks	**Body Weight in Pounds**									Sample Behavioral Effects
	90	100	120	140	160	180	200	220	240	
0	.00	.00	.00	.00	.00	.00	.00	.00	.00	Only completely safe limit
1	.05	.05	.04	.03	.03	.03	.02	.02	.02	Impairment begins
2	.10	.09	.08	.07	.06	.05	.05	.04	.04	Driving skills significantly affected; Information processing altered
3	.15	.14	.11	.10	.09	.08	.07	.06	.06	
4	.20	.18	.15	.13	.11	.10	.09	.08	.08	
5	.25	.23	.19	.16	.14	.13	.11	.10	.09	
6	.30	.27	.23	.19	.17	.15	.14	.12	.11	Legally intoxicated; Criminal penalties; Reaction time slowed; Loss of balance; Impaired movement; Slurred speech
7	.35	.32	.27	.23	.20	.18	.16	.14	.13	
8	.40	.36	.30	.26	.23	.20	.18	.17	.15	
9	.45	.41	.34	.29	.26	.23	.20	.19	.17	
10	.51	.45	.38	.32	.28	.25	.23	.21	.19	

One drink is 1.5 oz. shot of hard liquor, 12 oz. of beer or 5 oz. of table wine.

Subtract .015 for each hour that you take to consume the number of drinks listed in the table. For example, if you are a 160 pound woman and have two drinks in two hours, your BAC would be .06 - (2 x .015) = .03

NOTE: Blood Alcohol Level (BAL) charts do not take into consideration a wide range of additional variables that contribute to the determination of BAL's achieved and the behavioral effects experienced at a given BAL. These additional variables include: age, water-to-body-mass ratio, ethanol metabolism, tolerance level, drugs or medications taken, amount and type of food in the stomach during consumption, speed of consumption, and general physical condition. Thus, BAL charts only provide extremely rough estimates and should never be used alone to determine any individual's safe level of drinking.

Adapted from BAC Charts produced by the National Clearinghouse for Alcohol and Drug Information.

Table 1.3 Percentile Table for Alcohol Use

Drinks per week	Total	Men	Women
0	35	29	41
1	58	46	68
2	66	54	77
3	68	57	78
4	71	61	82
5	77	67	86
6	78	68	87
7	80	70	89
8	81	71	89
9	82	73	90
10	83	75	91
11	84	75	91
12	85	77	92
13	86	77	93
14	87	79	94
15	87	80	94
16	88	81	94
17	89	82	95
18	90	84	96
19	91	85	96
20	91	86	96
21	92	88	96
22	92	88	97
23–24	93	88	97
25	93	89	98
26–27	94	89	98
28	94	90	98
29	95	91	98
30–33	95	92	98
34-35	95	93	98
36	96	93	98
37–39	96	94	98
40	96	94	99
41–46	97	95	99
47–48	97	96	99
49–50	98	97	99
51–62	98	97	99
63–64	99	97	>99.5
65–84	99	98	>99.6
85–101	99	99	>99.9
102–159	>99.5	99	>99.9
160+	>99.8	>99.5	>99.9

Source: 1990 National Alcohol Survey, Alcohol Research Group, Berkeley. Courtesy of Dr. Robin Room.

Table 1.4 Common Effects of Different Levels of Intoxication

.02 – .06%	This is the "normal" social drinking range. Driving, even at these levels, is unsafe.
.08%	Memory, judgment, and perception are impaired. Legally intoxicated in most states.
.1%	Reaction time and coordination of movement are affected. Legally intoxicated in all states.
.15%	Vomiting may occur in normal drinkers; balance is often impaired.
.2%	Memory "blackout" may occur, causing loss of recall for events occurring while intoxicated.
.3%	Unconsciousness in a normal person, though some remain conscious at levels in excess of .6% if tolerance is very high.
.4 – .5%	Fatal dose for a normal person, though some survive higher levels if tolerance is very high.

Feedback Sheets

Following are copies of the Feedback Sheets you and your partner will complete in conjunction with your therapist.

Feedback Sheet 1

For the Drinker:

1. Based on the information I obtained during the assessment, I calculated the number of "standard drinks" you consumed in a typical week during the last 3 months before you came in :

    Total number of standard drinks per *week* ———————————

    Average number of standard drinks per *drinking day* ———————————

2. When we look at everyone who drinks in the United States, you have been drinking more than approximately —————— percent of the population in the country.

3. I also estimated your highest and average blood alcohol level (BAL) in the past 3 months. Your BAL is based on how many standard drinks you consume, the length of time over which you drink that much, whether you are a man or a woman, and how much you weigh. So,

    Your estimated *peak BAL* in the past 3 months was ———————————

    Your estimated *typical BAL* in an average week was ———————————

4. You have experienced many negative consequences from drinking. Here are some of the most important:

    ———————————————   ———————————————

    ———————————————   ———————————————

    ———————————————   ———————————————

Feedback Sheet 2

For the Partner:

1. Based on the information you provided during the assessment, you have made a number of attempts to support your partner in not drinking:

_____   _____

_____   _____

_____   _____

_____   _____

2. You've also reacted to your partner's drinking in a number of ways that probably have been less helpful:

_____   _____

_____   _____

_____   _____

_____   _____

Feedback Sheet 3

For the Couple:

1. The two of you both see certain problems or concerns about your relationship:

_____   _____

_____   _____

_____   _____

_____   _____

2. There are some problems or concerns, however, that one of you has emphasized more than the other:

Client's concerns: **Partner's concerns:**

_____   _____

_____   _____

_____   _____

_____   _____

Changing a habit like heavy drinking is difficult. You can help! Small things can help your partner keep trying. One thing you can do is to say pleasant things that show you notice your partner's efforts. Compliments have powerful effects on other people. Focus them on the positives (say "You look nice today") and avoid reminding your partner of the negatives (don't say "You don't look so puffy since you stopped drinking"). Talk together about pleasant things you can say to show your appreciation. Your words of encouragement can keep your partner going.

Often people say things to others and assume they are saying something nice. People make many mistakes when they assume something about another person. Other people do not always understand what we say. Everyone has an example of a time when they thought they said something positive but their comment was taken the wrong way. You will avoid trouble by asking your partner what he or she finds helpful. Develop a list of things that he or she would like to hear. Agree on three or four comments you will say to your partner for encouragement. Tell your partner that these are things that you will say as recognition for his or her efforts.

Do things to show your appreciation. Your actions will keep your partner going as well. Think of some small ways to show your appreciation. Leaving your partner a note, calling during the day, e-mailing, and bringing home something your partner likes can all help. Talk with your partner to find out what he or she would like. Don't assume that you know what your partner wants. Write a list of your ideas in the space provided and try them out.

Supporting Change

List 3 to 6 actions that you could do to support your partner in changing.

1. _____

2. _____

3. _____

4. _____

5. _____

6. _____

Some days you may find it hard to be supportive. You may start thinking of the problems your partner's drinking has caused. You may feel angry and resentful at times. These feelings are normal, but if you dwell on them they will only get worse. Remind yourself that your partner wants to change and is trying to change. If you help, you'll both get what you want in the end!

For the Client—Self-Monitoring

An important part of treatment is to work with facts and accurate information. In your case, your therapist will want to learn about what happens during your day.

The best way to collect facts is to write them down as they happen. Trying to recall things later is difficult. Everyone makes mistakes when they try to figure out what happened in the past, whether it was a few days ago or yesterday.

Self-monitoring is when you write down what you do during the day as it relates to your drinking. By recording your drinking and urges, your therapist will get a better idea of what is going on. Monitoring will help you and your therapist identify patterns in your life. Your monitoring records will help you realize the behavior chains that lead to drinking.

With self-monitoring, drinkers are surprised by how much they are drinking and that their drinking falls into patterns that happen over and over. Self-monitoring also helps you realize how often you are getting urges or desires to drink and what leads to these urges. It also helps you assess your satisfaction with your relationship and how, and if, it changes from day to day. Every relationship has good and bad days. You will see a general improvement in your relationship as this program continues. Overall, self-monitoring will help your therapist assess your progress over the duration of the program.

On the recording cards provided in the appendix at the end of the book, write down your urges to drink, any drinks you may have had, and how satisfied you are with your relationship for that particular day. You will need to do this on a daily basis. The appendix contains enough recording cards for 2 weeks. Please feel free to make photocopies as you will need additional cards as treatment progresses.

Your therapist can help you come up with a reminder system so that you remember to monitor your drinking and relationship satisfaction every day. You may keep your recording cards in a visible location in your home, such as on your bedside table or near the front door. When you have a drink or experience an

Daily monitoring							Date 10/8/08
Urges			**Drinks**				
Time	How strong? (1 – 7)	Trigger	Time	Type of drink	Amount (in ounces)	% Alcohol	Trigger
8:00 a.m.	4	Traffic during commute					
5:30 p.m.	7	Irritated when I came home	6:00 p.m.	Wine	1 bottle 25 oz.	12%	Fight with John
Relationship Satisfaction 1 2 ③ 4 5 6 7 very low greatest ever							
For woman only Do you have your menstrual period today? Yes (No) N/A							

Figure 1.1

Example of Completed Partner Self-Recording Card

urge, be sure to write it down as soon as possible. Don't rely on your memory later.

Figure 1.1 shows an example of a completed self-monitoring card. Review this sample along with the instructions for completing the card together with your partner and your therapist. Because self-monitoring is so important, it is essential that you understand exactly how it should be done. If you have questions, talk to your therapist.

Instructions for Self-Monitoring

The self-monitoring cards are an easy way to keep track of what is happening to your urges, drinking, and relationship satisfaction from day to day. Complete a card every day using the following instructions.

Date: Make sure to write in the date that you are filling in the card. You should fill in a card for every day of the week. The information from your cards will be used to identify patterns that emerge during the week.

Urges: Under the column marked "Urges," write down the time the urge occurred and how intense it was. For intensity, put down a number between one and seven to describe how strong the urge was. Number 1 would mean that the urge was very weak. Number seven would mean that the urge was one of the strongest that you have ever felt. If the urge was somewhere in the middle, then give it a number in between. Write down what triggered the urge.

Drinks: In the "Drinks" section, record information about what you drank, how much, and the amount of alcohol in the drink.

In the column labeled "Time," write down the time you started drinking.

In the column labeled "Type of Drink," write down the name of the drink you had (e.g., red wine, light beer, martini, etc.)

In the column labeled "Amount," write down how many drinks you had and the size of each drink. For example, the person who completed the sample recording card in Figure 1.1 says she drank a 750-ml bottle (a "fifth"). A 750-ml bottle has about 25 ounces of liquid. Maybe in your case, you would have had a drink with vodka in it. If so, you should estimate the amount of vodka in your cocktail. One way to do this is to know the size of the glass and how much liquid it holds. It is helpful to measure your drinks, so you can understand how much you're drinking.

In the column labeled "% Alcohol," write down the alcohol content of the drink you are having. Most times, this information can be found on the bottle or can.

In the column labeled "Trigger," list the event that led to the drinking.

Relationship Satisfaction: Write down how satisfied you are with your relationship each day. Use a number between 1 and 7 to rate your satisfaction. For example, if you are not satisfied at all with the relationship, circle 1. If you are extremely satisfied, circle 7. If you are in-between, pick a number somewhere in the middle.

Menstrual Period (for women only): Circle "Yes" if you are menstruating that day; circle "No" if you are not (or N/A if this does not apply to you).

For the Partner—Partner Monitoring Cards

The partner monitoring cards are an easy way to record what you observe. On these cards, you should write down what you see and how satisfied you are with your relationship. Some of the behaviors you should note are your partner's drinking, drug use, and urges for alcohol.

There is one card for each week. Twelve cards are provided in the appendix at the end of the book. This should be sufficient to last you over the duration of the program. If you need additional copies, however, please feel free to make photocopies. Figure 1.2 shows an example of a completed partner monitoring card.

Every day you will write down what you see and how you feel about your relationship. The monitoring will be most accurate if you complete the card every day using the following instructions.

Day/Date: Make sure to write in the date of when you are filling out the card.

Drinking: Circle the amount of drinking you think your partner did during the day. You may not always be sure; make your best guess. There are four different levels of drinking:

- NO—Circle NO if your partner did not drink that day.
- L—Circle L if your partner drank one or two drinks that day.
- M—Circle M if your partner drank three or four drinks that day.
- H—Circle H if your partner drank five or more drinks that day.

Drug use: If your partner used drugs that day, circle Y. If your partner does not use any drugs or did not use drugs on that day, circle N.

Partner monitoring

Day	Date	Drinking	Drug use	Urge intensity	Relationship satisfaction
Monday	10/6/08	NO L M (H)	Y (N)	0 1 2 3 4 5 (6) 7	1 2 (3) 4 5 6 7
Tuesday	10/7/08	NO L (M) H	Y (N)	0 1 2 3 (4) 5 6 7	1 2 3 4 (5) 6 7
Wednesday	10/8/08	NO L M (H)	Y (N)	0 1 2 3 4 (5) 6 7	1 2 (3) 4 5 6 7
Thursday	10/9/08	NO (L) M H	Y (N)	0 1 (2) 3 4 5 6 7	1 2 3 4 5 (6) 7
Friday	10/10/08	NO L M (H)	Y (N)	0 1 2 3 4 5 6 (7)	(1) 2 3 4 5 6 7
Saturday	10/11/08	NO L M (H)	Y (N)	0 1 2 3 4 5 6 (7)	(1) 2 3 4 5 6 7
Sunday	10/12/08	NO L M (H)	Y (N)	0 1 2 3 (4) 5 6 7	1 (2) 3 4 5 6 7

Figure 1.2

Example of Completed Partner Recording Card

Urge intensity: Circle a number that represents the intensity of urges to drink your partner experienced during the day. Use a number between 0 and 7 to indicate the intensity of the urges. For example, if your partner suffers no urges during the day, circle 0. If your partner's urges are extremely strong, then circle the 7. If the urges are not as great, then circle a number in between.

Relationship Satisfaction: Circle a number between 1 and 7 to show how satisfied you are with your relationship on that particular day. For example, if you are not satisfied at all with the relationship, circle 1. If you are extremely satisfied, then circle 7. If you are in-between, pick a number somewhere in the middle.

Your contribution is important to this treatment. Your therapist will use the information you provide to help your partner stop drinking. In addition, the information will be used to help improve your relationship. Remember to write down your observations every day!

Abstinence

The first step in treatment is helping you to actually stop drinking. Then, you will move on to learning skills to stay sober, prevent relapse, cope better with problems, etc.

There are several options for stopping your use of alcohol. Your therapist will review with you the following options:

1. inpatient detoxification

2. outpatient detoxification

3. going "cold turkey"

4. stopping on your own, with the help of the therapist

After discussing these options with your therapist, you will work together, along with your partner, to devise a plan for achieving abstinence. Record your ideas in the space provided on the next page.

Abstinence Plan

_____

_____

_____

_____

_____

_____

_____

_____

_____

_____

_____

_____

_____

_____

_____

High-Risk Situations for the Week

At the end of each session, you will spend some time discussing with your therapist any problem situations that you think might come up in the following week. As you progress through therapy, you will get better and better at anticipating and handling these. A "high-risk situation" is a situation in which you would find it very difficult not to drink.

Work with your therapist and partner to identify at least one high-risk situation coming up in the next week. Write down ideas about how to handle this situation on the High-Risk Situations worksheet. Use the back of your self-recording cards to record how you actually handled the anticipated situation, and write down any unexpected high-risk situations that may have arisen during the week.

High-Risk Situations

What high-risk situations do you think you may experience this week?

Situation 1:
How can you handle this situation?

a. _____

b. _____

c. _____

d. _____

Situation 2:
How can you handle this situation?

a. _____

b. _____

c. _____

d. _____

Situation 3:
How can you handle this situation?

a. _____

b. _____

c. _____

d. _____

Situation 4:
How can you handle this situation?

a. _____

b. _____

c. _____

d. _____

Homework

Client Homework

✎ If not done already, make an appointment with your physician to have a physical and get blood tests done to check liver function.

✎ Begin self-monitoring your alcohol use, urges (intensity, frequency), and relationship satisfaction using the recording cards in the appendix.

✎ Use the back of your recording cards to record any high-risk situations you encounter during the week and how you handled them.

Partner Homework

✎ Begin recording your partner's alcohol use, urges (intensity), and relationship satisfaction using the recording cards in the appendix.

✎ Implement the plan to support your partner.

Couple Homework

✎ Review the information in this chapter.

✎ Complete the Drinking Patterns Questionnaire (DPQ). Remember, answers to questions should address the drinker's patterns, not the partner's. Your therapist will distribute this questionnaire to both you and your partner at the end of Session 1.

Chapter 2

Session 2: *Functional Analysis / Noticing Positive Behavior*

Goals

- To begin tracking your progress

- To analyze the chain of events that maintains your drinking

- To begin noticing and recording nice things about each other

Graphing Progress

Together with your therapist, you will use the information from yours and your partner's completed self-recording cards to complete the graphs on the pages that follow. The first graph is the Alcohol Use and Urges Graph. On this graph, you will record the following information each week:

1. Total number of standard drinks you consumed for the week (add up the number of drinks)

2. Total number of urges to drink you experienced during the week (urge frequency) (count up the number of urges)

3. Average strength of your urges during the week (1–7) (add up the ratings for all the urges during the week and divide by the total number of urges)

The second graph is the Relationship Satisfaction Graph. On this graph, both you and your partner will record your levels of satisfaction with your relationship for the week. For this graph, add up the relationship satisfaction ratings for the week and divide by the number of days.

Be sure to complete these graphs every week. You will do this at the start of each session with your therapist.

Alcohol Use and Urges Graph

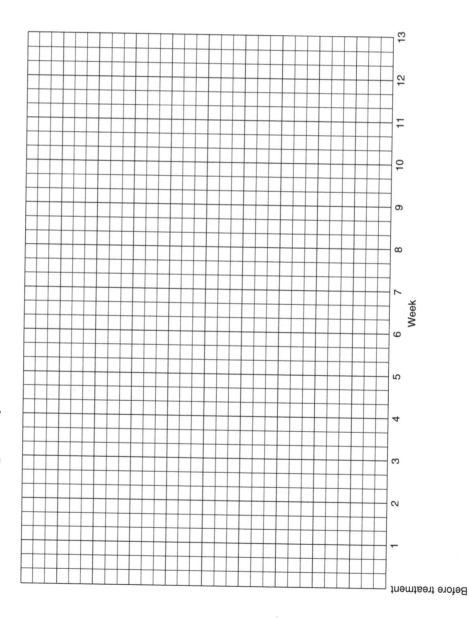

Week

Before treatment

Relationship Satisfaction Graph

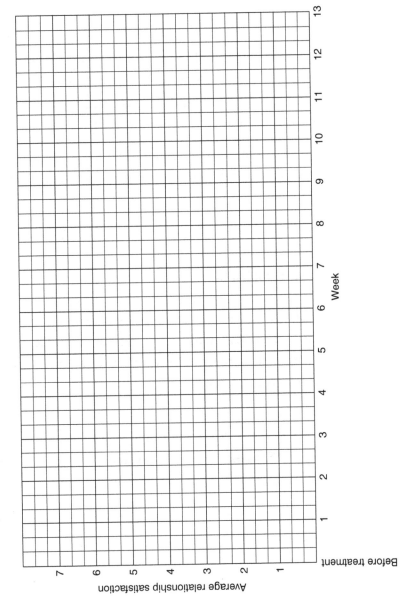

Functional Analysis

The first step in achieving abstinence is to understand more about your drinking. Together with your therapist, you will carefully identify and analyze all the factors that seem to be high-risk situations for you to drink. Then, you will put it all together to come up with a plan that will work for you. This is called a **functional analysis** or a habit analysis.

A functional analysis is a very important part of this treatment. It means looking at what happens before and after you drink. This helps us learn about the chains of events that keep your drinking going. Everyone has his or her own special type of behavior chain, but every chain can be looked at using the model shown in Figure 2.1 at the bottom of the page.

Every behavior chain follows a pattern: Triggers lead to thoughts and feelings that set up the drinker. After drinking, some good things happen (positive consequences) immediately and bad things (negative consequences) come later. Let's look at each step of the chain (see Table 2.1).

The first part of therapy is to conduct a functional analysis of what gets and keeps you drinking. Let's find out about your triggers. Later, you will learn new ways to break the chains.

The How-To's of Functional Analysis

Doing a functional analysis is just going back and figuring out the details of what happened when you drank. Start with one example, maybe the last time you drank, and look at the pattern or chain of events. A sample behavior chain is shown in Figure 2.2 on page 29.

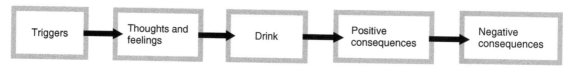

Figure 2.1
Drinking Behavior Chain

Table 2.1 Steps to Functional Analysis

Triggers	People, places, and things will be associated with drinking. A trigger is something that usually occurs before drinking. A trigger can be something easy to see or something sneaky. Often the drinker is not aware of the triggers. Triggers don't make people drink; they just set up thoughts and feelings connected to drinking.
Thoughts and feelings	Triggers set up thoughts and feelings. The triggers bring up feelings and ideas that are connected to drinking. These thoughts and feelings can be nice or unpleasant. Some examples are "I need to drink to be more sociable," "People will think I am weak if I don't drink," "Drinking will help me relax," or "Drinking will make me happy."
Drink	Drinking is something you do. It is a behavior that is a part of the chain.
Positive consequences	Very often something nice happens when someone drinks. The alcohol will often cause pleasant feelings. People learn to expect that alcohol will make them more relaxed, more sociable, or happy. These pleasant effects help keep people stuck on alcohol.
Negative consequences	The trouble that comes with alcohol often comes later. The trouble comes in many forms: arguments in the family, problems with a boss, financial difficulties, poor health, etc. Because the trouble comes later on, many people don't always make the connection between the trouble and their drinking. Many times, the possible trouble is out of your mind when thoughts of the pleasant parts of drinking are on your mind.

2 Trigger	3 Thoughts and feelings	1 Drink (when/where?)	4 Positive consequences	5 Negative consequences
Friday 5 pm, invitation from co-workers to go to sports bar	Tired and tense. "I deserve a break. I'll just have one quick drink and go home."	At sports bar Friday evening—stayed 2 1/2 hours, had 4 drinks instead of 1	Relaxation, initial euphoria from alcohol, socialize with friends, fun	Stayed too long, drank too much, spouse angry (argument followed), didn't see kids, drove under influence, had a hangover the next day

Figure 2.2

Example of Completed Behavior Chain

1. First, you write in the "Drink" column when and where the drinking happened. In our example, the person had four drinks at the sports bar Friday evening.

2. Then think back to what happened before the drinking happened. What were the people, places, or things that set up the drinking? Write these things in the "Trigger" column. In this example, the person had had a tough week and co-workers invited him out to a sports bar. Friday at 5 pm was also a trigger.

3. After writing the triggers, think back to those thoughts and feelings that made drinking more likely. In this example, the person thinks about being tired and tense after the work week, feels he deserves a break, and anticipates relaxation and fun at the bar.

4. After this, think about what happened after drinking. Remember the good things, the positive consequences. It is realistic to say that good things will happen, in the short term, to people when they drink. In our example, the person feels more relaxed, enjoys the initial euphoria from the alcohol, and enjoys socializing with his friends from work.

5. Now think about the things that happened later: the negative consequences. The problems created by drinking often come later on. In this example, our person had an argument with his wife, missed seeing his kids before bedtime, his driving was impaired, and he had a hangover the next day.

As with most people, the person in this example falls into a pattern. Some triggers will set off thoughts and emotions that lead to drinking. The drinking leads to some nice things happening. These nice things encourage the drinker to keep using alcohol.

The functional analysis helps us learn about patterns. Most people are not aware of the patterns and habits that happen in their lives, and it takes some detective work to identify these patterns.

Now it is your turn. To start, record your triggers in the space provided.

List of Triggers

Environmental (places, things)

_____

_____

_____

_____

Interpersonal (people)

_____

_____

_____

Emotions/Thoughts

_____

_____

_____

Physical

_____

_____

_____

_____

After you have started your list of triggers, work with your therapist to complete two behavior chains on the worksheet on the following page.

Behavior Chain

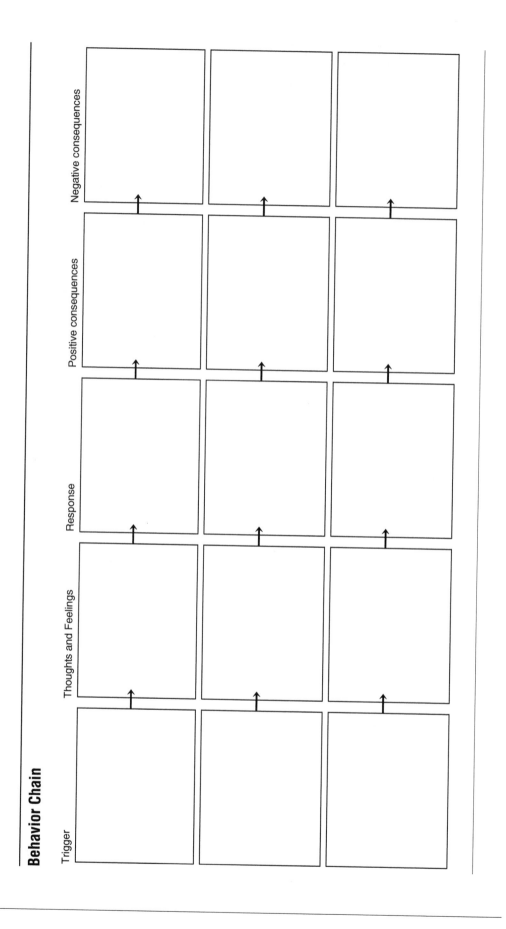

Trigger → Thoughts and Feelings → Response → Positive consequences → Negative consequences

Every day, we do hundreds of different things—getting up in the morning, getting dressed, making meals, going to work, watching TV, doing laundry, going to religious services, exercising—the list goes on and on. Many of the things we do have an impact on other people in our lives.

When couples are happy, they tend to notice the good things and overlook some of the bad. But, when couples are unhappy, they focus on the bad more than the good. In fact, unhappy couples are suspicious of good actions, and may think there's some bad motive behind them!

We've found that starting to focus on the positive can make a big difference. Just seeing the good things each day and looking for good actions can help you view your partner and your relationship in a different light.

Focusing on the positive doesn't mean you have no problems, and it won't make all your problems go away. But, if you realize there's a lot of good in your partner and in your relationship, it's easier to face the problems as well.

Each day, notice at least one good quality or action of your partner. Write it down. Don't tell your partner what you noticed, just keep track for yourself. You'll talk about them in the session.

What are examples of good things to write down?

Everyday actions that you're used to—he showers and dresses nicely; she makes dinner for everyone; he puts the toilet seat down; she mentions an interesting article in the newspaper; he puts the kids to bed; she reminds him that his mother's birthday is coming up.

Special actions — he pours her a cup of coffee and brings it to her; she picks up his cleaning for him; he does the laundry; she gives him a massage.

Anything that you think is nice, or that you appreciate about your partner that day.

Notice Something Nice

During the therapy session, you and your partner will use this worksheet to list some positive things you noticed about each other this week. For homework, you and your partner will record the positive things you notice about one another on a daily basis on the back of your self-recording cards.

1. Client—What nice things did your partner do this week?

_____

_____

_____

_____

2. Partner—What nice things did your partner do this week?

_____

_____

_____

_____

Work with your therapist and partner to identify at least one high-risk situation coming up in the next week. Write down ideas about how to handle this situation on the High-Risk Situations worksheet. Use the back of your self-recording card to record how you actually handled the anticipated situation, and write down any unexpected high-risk situations that may have come up during the week.

High-Risk Situations

What high-risk situations do you think you may experience this week?
Situation 1:

How can you handle this situation?
a.

_____

b.

_____

c.

_____

d.

_____

Situation 2:

How can you handle this situation?
a.

_____

b.

_____

c.

_____

d.

_____

Situation 3:

How can you handle this situation?
a.

_____

b.

_____

c.

_____

d.

_____

Situation 4:

How can you handle this situation?
a.

_____

b.

_____

c.

_____

d.

_____

Client Homework

✎ Continue self-recording. Remember to use the back of your self-recording cards to write down the ways you handled your high-risk situations for the week.

✎ If not completed in session, finish filling out your list of triggers.

✎ Complete two or more behavior chains in detail. Blank copies of the Behavior Chain worksheet can be found at the end of the chapter and in the appendix.

✎ Begin noticing and recording one positive partner action each day. Use the back of your self-recording cards.

Partner Homework

✎ Continue recording your partner's alcohol use, urges (intensity), and your level of relationship satisfaction.

✎ Continue supportive comments and actions.

✎ Begin noticing and recording one positive partner action each day. Use the back of your recording cards.

Couple Homework

✎ Review the information in this chapter.

Behavior Chain

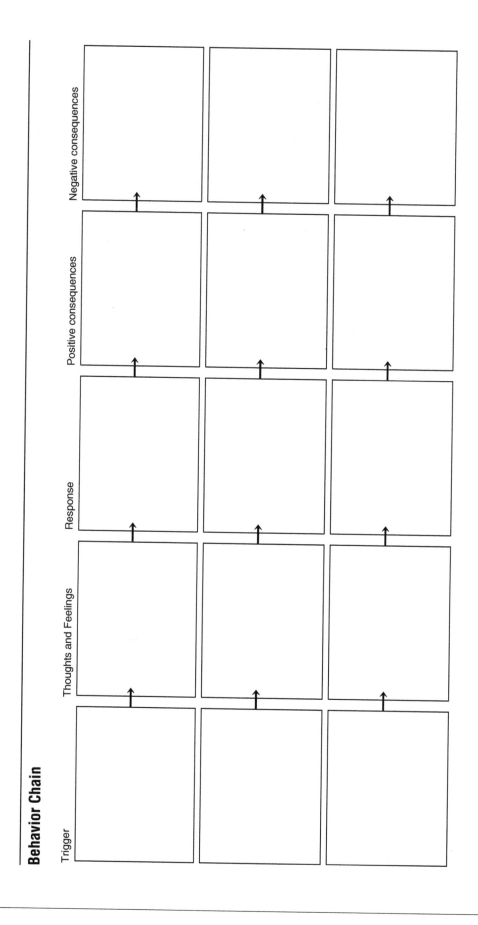

Behavior Chain

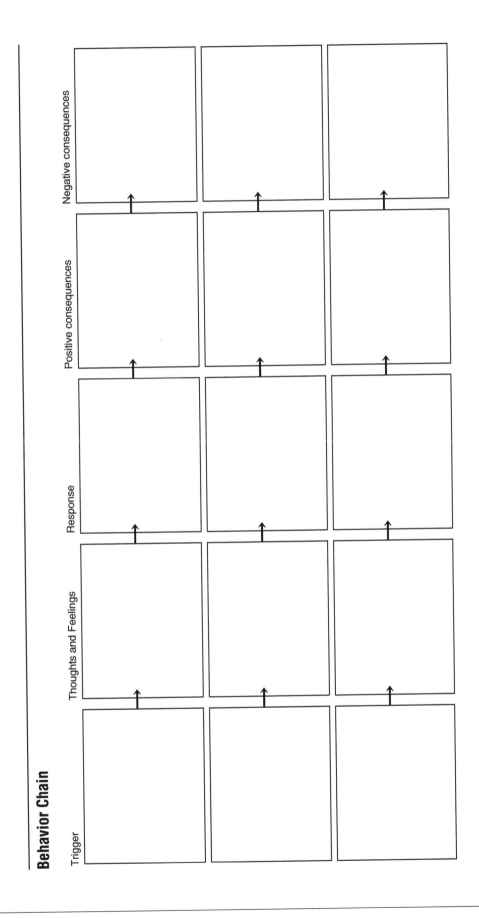

Chapter 3

Session 3: High-Risk Hierarchy / Partner Functional Analysis Part I / Self-Management Plans

Goals

- To identify your high-risk situations and list them in order of difficulty

- For your partner to complete a functional analysis of behaviors that may serve as triggers for your drinking

- To develop a plan for dealing with the triggers for your drinking

Graphing Progress

As you have done every week, be sure to update your Alcohol Use and Urges and Relationship Satisfaction graphs in Chapter 2 using the information from your most recently completed self-recording cards.

Looking Ahead for Trouble

Last week, you identified some of the major situations, feelings, people, and behaviors that are associated with your drinking. This week, your therapist is going to help you plan for these difficulties.

Smart travelers look ahead for possible trouble. By looking ahead for rough spots in the road, they can handle tough situations better. Travelers who see the trouble ahead on the road can make changes to steer around the problem. In the same way, people who quit drinking can look ahead for difficult situations. Smart people plan for the rough spots.

Everybody who has stopped drinking has faced people, places, or things that made it difficult to stay sober. Some situations are more difficult than others.

For you, some situations will be easier to handle. Other situations will be more difficult to manage.

What are your rough spots? What people, places, emotions, or things can be trouble for you? What are your triggers for drinking? You made a list of these last week. Look back to Chapter 2 for your list, and add anything new that you noticed this week. Think of what goes with drinking:

- People

- Places

- Things you see, like bottles

- Problems with your partner

- Emotions, like sadness, anger, boredom, and happiness

- Problems with your children

- Good times

- Events, like parties

Some rough spots are harder and others are easier to handle. You can usually tell ahead of time how hard something will be. By thinking about how hard different situations can be, you can be ready for the tougher ones.

Now go back to your list of triggers from Chapter 2. For each trigger listed, think about how easy or difficult it would be to avoid drinking when that particular trigger comes up. Arrange your triggers from the hardest to the easiest on the High-Risk Hierarchy provided.

Then, rate how hard each situation is for you. The easiest way to do this is by using numbers. Use numbers between 0 and 100 to describe each situation. Larger numbers mean that the situation is harder to handle. Smaller numbers mean that the situation is easier. Something that is no trouble at all would get a number 0. Something that would be very hard for you to handle would get a higher number. A rating of 100 would mean that the situation was the most difficult one for you to handle without drinking. Figure 3.1 shows a sample High-Risk Hierarchy.

Difficult situation	How hard?
Being angry after an argument with my partner	95
Being at a party with alcohol	85
Working on the yard	85
Co-workers going out for drinks invite me	80
My partner yelling at me for drinking	75
Being at a professional meeting	65
Watching TV	55

Figure 3.1

Sample High-Risk Hierarchy

Now it is your turn to create a hierarchy. Use the worksheet on the next page to put your high-risk situations in order from hardest to easiest.

High-Risk Hierarchy

Difficult Situation	How Hard?	
	Very easy (0)	Very hard (100)

Some high-risk situations for drinking may come from things that you do. You are not to blame for your partner's drinking, and he or she always has responsibility for drinking or not drinking. But, there are things that you may do that are triggers for your partner's drinking—that is, they increase his or her desire to drink. You also react to your partner's drinking. Some of your reactions may protect your partner from experiencing negative consequences that otherwise would occur, while others may be positive consequences for drinking, even though you don't want them to be.

Spouses/significant others have a big effect on a person's drinking.

- They may do things that are upsetting to their partner and "trigger" his or her desire to drink.

- They may care about their partner and want to protect him or her from the bad things that might happen when he or she drinks.

- And, they sometimes do things that make drinking enjoyable.

- All of these actions can make the problem worse, but none of them caused the drinking problem, and your partner is always responsible for his or her own actions. But, you can help by changing your own reactions and by recognizing that you are responsible for your own actions.

Let's start with some examples that illustrate a person's effect on his partner's drinking:

Case Example 1

Robert comes home from work and finds the kids playing unsupervised and Nancy lying on the couch drunk. He gets mad and yells at her and she goes upstairs to drink more. He makes dinner for the kids and then feels guilty for having yelled at his partner. He brings her dinner in bed.

In this example, Robert's complaining about irresponsibility because of drinking is a trigger for further drinking. This is a partner-related trigger. After drinking, short-term positive consequences for Nancy include avoiding making dinner, not being bothered by the children, and getting dinner in bed. Long-term negative consequences include feeling depressed, guilty, and angry with herself for having

Trigger	Thoughts and feelings	Behavior	Positive consequences	Negative consequences
Robert calls me irresponsible.	He's right. I'm a horrible mother.	Drink alone, upstairs.	Robert makes dinner. I have no responsibilities for a while.	Depressed, guilty, and angry with myself. Robert is very angry.

Figure 3.2

Nancy's Behavior Chain

no self-control over drinking and being lazy and not spending time with the children. Here is what Nancy's behavior chain would look like (see Figure 3.2).

Case Example 2

Jane hasn't been drinking for about two months. John's company picnic is coming up and he suggests that they go. Jane doesn't know many people, and feels very uncomfortable there. They join up with a group of John's co-workers and their wives for dinner, and everyone is drinking beers or wine coolers. Someone offers Jane a wine cooler and she drinks it, and then three more. She feels upset and disappointed with herself, but on the way home, all John talks about is what a great time they had. She feels terrible and continues to drink after they get home.

In this example, John's taking Jane to the picnic was a trigger for drinking. His lack of awareness of her distress was also a trigger for additional drinking. Being offered the wine cooler was the third part of the trigger. Positive consequences of drinking were that Jane felt like she was part of the group. Negative consequences include her disappointment with herself and her anger at John for being unaware of the difficulty she had had. Here is what Jane's behavior chain would look like (see Figure 3.3).

Triggers	Thoughts and feelings	Behavior	Positive consequences	Negative consequences
Company picnic. Someone gives me a wine cooler. John's talking with his buddies.	Uncomfortable Angry at John What's the use?	Drink 4 wine coolers	Feel more comfortable at picnic	Keep drinking at home Still angry Broke my sobriety John doesn't understand

Figure 3.3

Jane's Behavior Chain

Figure out which actions of yours might trigger your partner's desire to drink. You can ask your partner for input if you feel comfortable. List these on the Partner-Related Triggers and Consequences worksheet provided.

Think about the ways you have protected your partner in the past—by taking care of him or her when he or she was drinking, by covering up for your partner with friends or family, by picking up your partner's responsibilities, etc. Add these to the list of protecting actions.

Think about ways you might have provided positive consequences when your partner drank—by having a few drinks with him or her, having a good time at a party or with friends and letting your partner know it was fun, or by trying to be nice and not making waves when your partner was drinking. Add these to the list.

Partner-Related Triggers and Consequences

Actions of mine that might be triggers for_____ 's drinking:

_____

_____

_____

_____

Actions of mine that might be positive consequences for _____ 's drinking:

_____

_____

_____

_____

Actions of mine that might protect _____ from the consequences of drinking:

_____

_____

_____

_____

In this program, you have spent some time talking about your triggers. Triggers come in all shapes and sizes. Some lead to very strong urges, while others lead to very difficult situations. Some are easier to handle than others. Some involve loved ones; others come from your daily routine.

- Knowing about triggers is not enough. You need a plan!

- Developing a good plan takes patience and a lot of thinking. This program will teach you a step-by-step method that makes planning much easier.

- There are both your personal triggers and other triggers related to your relationship.

Follow these steps for designing a plan for managing your triggers:

1. Pick out triggers that you will come across soon. Start with an easier trigger. As you get more practice at this, you can plan for harder triggers.

2. Write down as many ideas as possible for handling the trigger. Be creative! Do not worry about being silly or unrealistic. The best ideas often come when you let ideas fly without stopping to think about what is good or bad about each one. The evaluation will come later. There are three kinds of strategies for handling triggers:

   - Remove yourself from the situation to avoid trouble.
   - Change things around you to avoid the trigger. For example, get rid of alcohol around the house or do not walk past the liquor store.
   - Think or act in different ways when you are faced with the trigger. For example, someone may avoid drinking by remembering the consequences that will come later.

3. After coming up with a lot of ideas, think about them all and write down what is good and bad about each one. Now is the time to think about what you need to do for each one of the ideas. Remember, some consequences of your plan will happen quickly and others will happen later. Try to think them through. The goal here is to think about what is good and bad about each idea.

4. Think about how easy or hard each idea would be for you. Some ideas will be hard to do, others will be easy. For each idea or plan, give it a number between 1 and 10 that shows how hard it would be to do. For example, the easiest plan that you can do would get a 1. The hardest thing that you could

ever do would get a 10. Write down how hard each idea would be for you. That is, how difficult would it be to carry out the new plan in place of old behavior that involved drinking in response to the same trigger?

5. Pick a plan. Choose the plan or plans that have the best balance between positive and negative consequences. Try to pick ones that will not be too hard for you.

6. After putting a plan to work, check to see how it is working. If a plan is not working, do not be afraid to make changes or to pick another idea.

Now it's your turn. Use the Self-Management Planning Sheet to write down your top triggers for drinking (refer to your completed High-Risk Hierarchy) and build your plan for dealing with them. We have provided a sample plan for you to use as a model when designing your own (see Figure 3.4).

Trigger	Plan	+\−Consequences	Difficulty (1–10)
Going to a restaurant for lunch	1. Don't eat lunch	+ Avoid trigger	9
		− Will be hungry	
	2. Eat lunch at work	+ Avoid trigger + Won't be hungry + Will save money	5
		− Boring	
	3. Go to a restaurant that doesn't serve liquor	+ Avoid trigger	3
		− Co-workers may not agree − Loss of privacy	
	4. Learn to refuse when co-workers urge me to order a drink	+ Don't need to switch restaurants	8
		− May feel uncomfortable − Loss of privacy − Still faced with difficult trigger	
Keeping liquor in the house	1. Never buy liquor	+ Save money + Avoid trigger	5
		− Partner can't drink at home − Company can't drink	
	2. Hide the liquor	+ Avoid trigger	9
		− Inconvenient − I can find it	
	3. Don't invite people over who drink	+ Avoid trigger	8
		− Lose friends	
	4. Don't serve liquor to guests	+ Save money + Put myself first	7
		− Some people may be offended	
	5. Buy liquor right before guests arrive and throw out the extra after they leave	+ Avoid offending guests + Minimize exposure to trigger	2
		− May waste money	

Figure 3.4

Example of Completed Self-Management Planning Sheet

Self-Management Planning Sheet

Trigger	Plan	+\−Consequences	Difficulty (1–10)
I.			
2.			

Work with your therapist and partner to identify at least one high-risk situation coming up in the next week. Write down ideas about how to handle this situation on the High-Risk Situations worksheet. Use the back of your self–recording card to record how you actually handled the anticipated situation, and write down any unexpected high-risk situations that may have arisen during the week.

High-Risk Situations

What high-risk situations do you think you may experience this week?

Situation 1:
How can you handle this situation?

a. _____

b. _____

c. _____

d. _____

Situation 2:
How can you handle this situation?

a. _____

b. _____

c. _____

d. _____

Situation 3:
How can you handle this situation?

a. _____

b. _____

c. _____

d. _____

Situation 4:
How can you handle this situation?

a. _____

b. _____

c. _____

d. _____

Client Homework

✎ Continue self-recording. Remember to use the back of your self-recording cards to write down the ways you handled your high-risk situations for the week.

✎ Record one positive partner action each day on the back of your self-recording cards.

✎ Finish creating your hierarchy of high-risk situations if not completed in the session.

✎ Complete a self-management plan for two of your drinking triggers. A blank copy of the Self-Management Planning Sheet is provided at the end of the chapter, as well as in the appendix.

✎ Choose two times during the week when you had a "strong urge" to drink and develop a behavior chain for each. A blank Behavior Chain worksheet is provided at the end of the chapter, as well as in the appendix.

Partner Homework

✎ Continue recording your partner's alcohol use, urges (intensity), and your level of relationship satisfaction.

✎ Record one positive partner action each day on the back of your partner recording cards.

✎ Finish filling out the Partner-Related Triggers and Consequences worksheet if not completed in session.

Couple Homework

✎ Review the information in this chapter.

Self-Management Planning Sheet

Trigger	Plan	+\−Consequences	Difficulty (1–10)
I.			
2.			

Behavior Chain

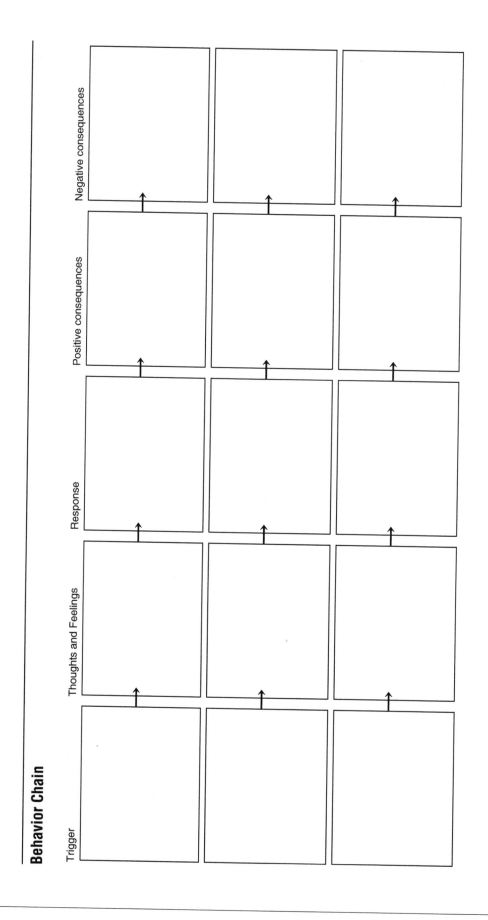

Chapter 4

*Session 4: Partner Functional Analysis
Part II / Enhancing Motivation to Change*

Goals

- To work out a self-management plan for another trigger from your High-Risk Hierarchy

- To work together with your partner to devise a plan for handling alcohol in the house

- To think about your reasons for wanting to quit drinking

Graphing Progress

As you have done every week, be sure to update your Alcohol Use and Urges and Relationship Satisfaction graphs in Chapter 2 using the information from your most recently completed self-recording cards.

Self-Management Planning

Choose another trigger from your High-Risk Hierarchy, one rated as more difficult than the one you did last week, and work out a self-management plan for that trigger using the Self-Management Planning Sheet on the next page.

Self-Management Planning Sheet

Trigger	Plan	+/−Consequences	Difficulty (1–10)
1.			
2.			

Alcohol in the House Planning

One type of situation that partners often are concerned about is having alcohol in the house. Some partners would like to keep alcohol in the house to be able to have an occasional drink him or herself or to serve when company is over. Other times, a partner will be concerned that the stocked liquor cabinet or beer in the refrigerator is just too much of a trigger for drinking. Some problem drinkers feel similarly; others find that alcohol in the house does not make much difference. Have you and your partner thought about this? Have you discussed it with each other at all?

Try to come to a decision with you partner about how you will handle alcohol in the house and write down your plan in the space provided.

Alcohol in the House

_____

_____

_____

_____

_____

_____

_____

_____

Even though you have entered treatment, you probably have some mixed feelings about being in therapy and about actually making major changes in your life. This is a common feeling. You don't know what things will be like in the future, and that makes it somewhat frightening. In contrast, you do know what things are like now. Sometimes the familiar is comforting, even if it is unhappy. You are also giving up something that has provided good things in your life. Most people get pleasure from drinking—they enjoy the taste, like the sensations, and associate it with many good things in their lives. Giving it up is like saying good-bye to a friend you will miss, even though you know that alcohol is not a friend that has your best interests in mind. Having mixed feelings about giving up alcohol is perfectly natural.

You may also have mixed feelings about abstinence. Some people feel that it's impossible to have fun without alcohol or feel that it's the only way they can relax.

Review the section that follows and think about some of the pros and cons of drinking and not drinking. In thinking about the pros and cons, it may be helpful to think about short-term consequences and long-term consequences.

The Good, the Bad, and the Ugly of Drinking

STOP! Why do you want to quit drinking?

Before moving on, look at the good and bad things about your drinking. You probably have mixed feelings about stopping your drinking. It will help to stay motivated if you know why you wish to quit.

Think about the things that happen when you drink. These things are called consequences. Some consequences are good and others are bad. Most of the time, the good consequences happen right when you are drinking, and the bad consequences come later.

There are reasons why you drink. These come from the good things that happen, even if the good things only happen sometimes. Your mind and body remember these things.

The bad consequences can come right when you are drinking (like getting sick or having a fight) or can come later (like not being able to get up the next morning or having your children upset with you).

It will be easier to quit if you have a list of the bad things about drinking. The more you remember the bad things, the easier it is to say no when you have an urge to drink.

Also think about what's good and bad about quitting drinking. Some people don't think ahead when they make a change in their life. You will be more successful if you look ahead to see the good and bad about making a change. Thinking about what you lose and what you get makes it easier to stay motivated.

Take a moment and start writing down the things that happen to you when you drink. Write down the things that happen right away and the things that happen later. Examples of consequences are:

- Physical effects: body sensations, getting sick, headaches, etc.

- Negative feelings

- Depressing thoughts

- Things that happen with other people, such as family or friends

- Money or legal trouble

- Work problems

On the Decisional Matrix sheet provided, write down the good and bad things that happen right away (immediate consequences) when you drink. Also write down the good and bad things that happen later (delayed consequences) after drinking. Write these in the section marked "Continued Alcohol Use."

Do the same thing for quitting drinking. Write down the good and bad things that will happen right away when you stop drinking. Then write down the good and bad things that will come to you later. Write these in the section marked "Abstinence."

Remember to be realistic! It is important to be honest. The more you understand the reasons why you drink, the easier it will be to find a solution. When you are done, you should have more good reasons for stopping drinking than for keeping things the way they are.

Decisional Matrix

Abstinence

Pros (short- and long-term)

_____

_____

_____

_____

_____

_____

_____

Cons (short- and long-term)

_____

_____

_____

_____

_____

_____

_____

Continued Alcohol Use

Pros (short- and long-term)

_____

_____

_____

_____

_____

_____

_____

Cons (short- and long-term)

_____

_____

_____

_____

_____

_____

_____

High-Risk Situations for the Week

Work with your therapist and partner to identify at least one high-risk situation coming up in the next week. Write down ideas about how to handle this situation on the High-Risk Situations worksheet. Use the back of your self-recording card to record how you actually handled the anticipated situation, and write down any unexpected high-risk situations that may have arisen during the week.

High-Risk Situations

What high-risk situations do you think you may experience this week?

Situation 1:

How can you handle this situation?

a.

_____

b.

_____

c.

_____

d.

_____

Situation 2:

How can you handle this situation?

a.

_____

b.

_____

c.

_____

d.

_____

Situation 3:

How can you handle this situation?

a.

_____

b.

_____

c.

_____

d.

_____

Situation 4:

How can you handle this situation?

a.

_____

b.

_____

c.

_____

d.

_____

Client Homework

✎ Continue self-recording. Remember to use the back of your self-recording cards to write down the ways you handled your high-risk situations for the week.

✎ Record one positive partner action each day on the back of your self-recording cards.

✎ Complete self-management plans for triggers not yet addressed. Blank copies of the Self-Management Planning Sheet are provided at the end of the chapter.

✎ Finish filling out the Decisional Matrix if not completed in session.

✎ Implement self-management plans and write on the back of your self-recording cards how you dealt with the triggers.

Partner Homework

✎ Continue recording your partner's alcohol use, urges (intensity), and your level of relationship satisfaction.

✎ Record one positive partner action each day on the back of your partner recording cards.

Couple Homework

✎ Review the information in this chapter.

✎ Implement your plan for keeping (or not keeping) alcohol in the house.

Self-Management Planning Sheet

Trigger	Plan	+/−Consequences	Difficulty (1–10)
1.			
2.			

Self-Management Planning Sheet

Trigger	Plan	+/−Consequences	Difficulty (1–10)
I.			
2.			

Chapter 5   *Session 5: Dealing with Urges / Decreasing Partner Triggers*

Goals

- To learn ways of coping with your urges to drink

- To review the skills you have learned and the progress you have made up to this point

Graphing Progress

As you have done every week, be sure to update your Alcohol Use and Urges and Relationship Satisfaction graphs in Chapter 2 using the information from your most recently completed self-recording cards.

Coping With Desires to Drink

This week, your therapist will offer you some ways to handle urges to drink.

Most people have urges to drink when they first quit. In the beginning, these urges happen often and can get very intense. The good news: After a while, the urges get easier to ignore.

Here are some things to remember about urges and triggers:

- Urges are reactions to triggers. Your body has learned to connect certain people, places, and things to drinking. The triggers can even be thoughts or emotions.

- Urges are a sign that you have to do something different. Something in the situation is making it difficult for you. The way you handle the situation has to change.

- Urges to drink don't last forever! They are like waves in the ocean—they peak, they crest, and they subside. They usually go away in a short time.

Even though the few minutes can seem very long, remember that the desire to drink will go away if you give it time.

Here are some ways to deal with an urge. Pick one or more that will work for you:

- Remind yourself that the urge is a temporary thing. No matter how bad it is, it will not last forever.

- If possible, get away from the situation that created the trigger.

- Go through the list of reasons why you decided to stop drinking. Remind yourself about the bad parts of drinking. Remind yourself about the good things about not drinking.

- Find something to do that will get your mind off the urge to drink. A fun activity that does not involve drinking will help distract you from the struggle.

- Talk with someone who is understanding. Often just talking about the urge will take some pressure off you.

- Say encouraging things to yourself that make you feel good about not drinking.

- Use your imagination. Imagine yourself in a pleasant place where you are peaceful and happy.

- Another way to use your imagination is to have a picture in your head of the urge looking like an ugly monster. Think of yourself as a ninja or a samurai fighting back and beating the monster. Or picture bleach poured in a wineglass.

- Imagine that you are in a boat and the urge is a big wave that comes and rocks the boat, but then passes you by.

- Tell yourself you can't always control when an urge comes, but you can just accept that "there's that urge again," and let it stay until it evaporates. Don't try to get rid of it, just kind of ignore it, distract yourself, and it will go away eventually.

- Pray.

These are some techniques used by people to fight off the urges. We give you a list because we know that everyone is different. However, we know that people have used these techniques to be successful.

Remember, urges get weaker over time. You will gain more confidence and pride in your ability to beat them.

Write down some ideas for dealing with your urges in the space provided.

Dealing With Urges

In response to an urge or craving to drink, I can . . .

_____

_____

_____

_____

_____

_____

For the Partner—Dealing With Urges—You Can Help

Remember:

- Urges are a normal part of stopping drinking

- Urges are reactions to triggers

- Urges do not mean that your partner:
  is a failure,
  will drink,
  will not be successful

They simply mean that your partner needs to cope with a trigger.

Your partner is learning many ways to cope with urges and you can help!

- Sometimes you can help by listening

- Sometimes there is something you can say that will help—just ask!

- Sometimes there is something you can do—get your partner a soft drink or a cup of tea; go for a walk together

Be sure to *ask* your partner what would help.

You may feel anxious or angry when your partner has an urge to drink. If this happens:

- Remind yourself that urges are normal

- Take a deep breath and calm yourself if you need to

- Keep your eye on your goals—a sober partner and a happier family

- And most important, remember to take care of yourself!

For the Partner—Coping With Urges

Use the following worksheet to brainstorm ideas of ways you can help your partner deal with urges to drink.

When my partner has an urge to drink I can:

_____

_____

_____

_____

_____

_____

_____

When my partner has an urge to drink I shouldn't:

_____

_____

_____

_____

_____

_____

_____

For the Partner—Changing Your Triggers for Your Partner's Drinking

In earlier sessions, you listed some of your actions that were triggers for your partner's drinking. Now we're ready for action!

Your partner has already started using self-management planning to deal with some of his or her triggers for drinking. Your therapist will help you use the same approach.

Here are the basics:

- Write down as many ideas as possible for changing how you handle a specific situation. Be creative! Don't worry about how good the idea is—you need to start with ideas.

- Look at the pros and cons of each idea—think about how comfortable you are with the idea, if it would help reduce the trigger and if there'd be a "cost" that you didn't like.

- For each idea, think about these pros and cons, and rate how difficult it would be for you to carry out each idea.

- Pick a plan. Choose the plan or plans that seem to have the best balance of positives and negatives.

- Put your plans into action, and see how they work.

Here are some examples (see Figure 5.1).

Now it's your turn. Use the Partner Self-Management Planning Sheet to write down some triggers for your partner's drinking that you want to change and build your plan for dealing with them.

Trigger	Plan	+/− Consequences	Difficulty (1 – 10)
Ordering a bottle of our favorite wine in a restaurant	Order a glass just for myself	+ I enjoy the wine	2
		− My partner has to see me drink	
	Ask my partner if she's comfortable with my ordering wine	+ We'd be communicating	3
		− My partner may be uncomfortable and I won't get to drink	3
	Order a different alcoholic beverage	+ My partner would be more comfortable	2
		− The drink may still serve as a trigger	
	Order a non-alcoholic beverage	+ I'd be supporting my partner	5
		− I might feel resentful	
Giving my partner very limited amounts of money so she won't spend it on liquor, which makes her feel bad and increases her desire to drink	Give my partner money for the week	+ It's what I normally do	9
		− I will be fearful that my partner will use the money for alcohol	
	Tell my partner that I'm worried she will use the money for alcohol	+ Feels good to be honest	5
		− Will hurt my partner's feelings	
	Give my partner enough money for a couple of days and increase the amount based on my partner's ability to stay sober	+ I will worry less	2
		− My partner may feel like I'm treating her like a child	
	Give the money to my partner's mother to manage	+ I wouldn't be the "bad guy"	10
		− My partner would be very upset	

Figure 5.1

Sample Partner Self-Management Planning Sheet

Partner Self-Management Planning Sheet

Trigger	Plan	+/−Consequences	Difficulty (1–10)
1.			
2.			

Review the following information with your therapist to highlight your progress over the past few weeks, as well as the new skills you've learned. This section also lists the topics you have yet to cover as part of the treatment program. This is to give you the "big picture" of the treatment plan and to help you see how much progress you've made here and how many new skills you now have under your belt.

For the Client

You have already learned a great deal in treatment. You have been practicing many skills to help keep you from drinking. You have been doing self-recording, learning to recognize your triggers, and gaining insight into the behavior chain that leads to drinking after one of your triggers happens.

You've learned what cues in the world start you feeling and thinking about drinking. You've figured out which risky situations are going to be the toughest for you—and since forewarned is forearmed, now you can be prepared. And you have learned to see ahead of time that these situations are coming up, so now you can plan accordingly. You'll see the trouble before you are right on top of it! You've learned to generate plans for dealing with triggers so that you are prepared with a specific way to deal with each trigger.

You have considered the pros and cons of drinking and of abstinence so that you may feel more strongly that the pros of abstinence outweigh the pros of drinking. You are also clearer on the cons of drinking.

You have some new tools to deal with urges and cravings.

For the Partner

You've learned a lot about what your partner is doing to deal with his or her drinking problem. Understanding more about drinking and how to change can make it easier for you to support your spouse/significant other.

You've been keeping track of your partner's drinking and urges and understand more about what triggers are hard for him or her to handle.

You've also learned about your own actions—things you do that make it easier or harder for your partner to stay sober. Now we're starting to think about how to change what you do. And you've been focusing on being supportive—giving your partner the encouragement he or she needs to face this difficult problem

For the Couple

You've just started in building a better relationship. You've started to notice nice things that your partner does and are leaning how to express your appreciation for those nice things.

You've started to learn . . .

- How to talk together to solve problems related to drinking

- What to do about having alcohol in the house

- How to work together when drinking urges occur.

You're on your way!

Stay tuned . . . Together, you'll be learning to:

- Create more rewards for sobriety to replace the positive consequences of drinking

- Know more about the negative consequences of drinking

- Challenge thoughts about alcohol that get you into trouble

- Deal effectively with situations where alcohol is present

- Make safer decisions

- Share more enjoyable activities

- Communicate with each other more effectively

- Solve problems effectively

- Identify warning signs that could lead to relapses

- Avoid relapses and deal with any slips

High-Risk Situations for the Week

Work with your therapist and partner to identify at least one high-risk situation coming up in the next week. Write down ideas about how to handle this situation on the High-Risk Situations worksheet. Use the back of your self-recording card to record how you actually handled the anticipated situation, and write down any unexpected high-risk situations that may have arisen during the week.

High-Risk Situations

What high-risk situations do you think you may experience this week?

Situation 1:
How can you handle this situation?

a.

_____

b.

_____

c.

_____

d.

_____

Situation 2:
How can you handle this situation?

a.

_____

b.

_____

c.

_____

d.

_____

Situation 3:
How can you handle this situation?

a.

_____

b.

_____

c.

_____

d.

_____

Situation 4:
How can you handle this situation?

a.

_____

b.

_____

c.

_____

Client Homework

✎ Continue self-recording. Remember to use the back of your self-recording cards to write down the ways you handled your high-risk situations for the week.

✎ Complete two more self-management plans for more difficult items on your High-Risk Hierarchy. A blank copy of the Self-Management Planning Sheet is provided at the end of the chapter.

✎ Use urge coping twice during the week in a high-risk situation or another time when experiencing an urge.

Partner Homework

✎ Continue recording your partner's alcohol use, urges (intensity), and your level of relationship satisfaction.

✎ Develop two self-management plans for your triggers for your partner's drinking. A blank copy of the Partner Self-Management Planning Sheet is provided at the end of the chapter, as well as in the appendix.

Couple Homework

✎ Review the information in this chapter.

✎ Practice at least one urge discussion during the week.

Self-Management Planning Sheet

Trigger	Plan	+/−Consequences	Difficulty (1–10)
I.			
2.			

Partner Self-Management Planning Sheet

Trigger	Plan	+/−Consequences	Difficulty (1–10)
1.			
2.			

Chapter 6

Session 6: Rearranging Behavioral Consequences / Shared Activities

Goals

- To learn ways of increasing the positive rewards of staying sober
- To discover alternative activities that you can engage in instead of drinking

Graphing Progress

As you have done every week, be sure to update your Alcohol Use and Urges and Relationship Satisfaction graphs in Chapter 2 using the information from your most recently completed self-recording cards.

Rearranging Behavioral Consequences

This week, you will learn ways to increase the positive rewards you experience from staying sober. You are also going to learn about other ways to increase the positive thoughts that you have about staying sober and increase the negative thoughts that you have right now about drinking.

Refer back to your completed Decisional Matrix from Chapter 4 and review the reasons you want to quit drinking and the consequences associated with drinking. Since it has been 2 weeks since you've completed the matrix, it makes sense to review it now and make any necessary changes/additions. You will discuss with your therapist the following two ways that you can use your matrix to help you become or stay sober.

Thinking Through the Drink

Before you drink, it is likely that you think about the short-term positive consequences of drinking. What you should begin doing is thinking about the negative consequences of drinking before you drink. The following exercise will help you start getting used to thinking about the cons of drinking, rather than the pros. This is one way of controlling your thoughts to help you avoid drinking.

Review your Decisional Matrix and the negative consequences of drinking that you listed. Write these consequences on a 3 × 5 index card and display it somewhere where you will see it often. Read it whenever you find yourself faced with a high-risk situation. For example, if some friends call and invite you and your partner to meet them at a club or bar, your first thoughts will probably be related to the positive consequences of going out and getting a drink. Instead of giving your friends an answer right away, delay accepting their offer and review your index card. Practice your new thinking habit. Then, call back and decline the invitation, using these suggestions:

- Be firm but polite—make it clear that you mean what you say when you decline.

- Suggest an alternative—Even though you aren't going to go to the club, say you'd like to see them and you wonder if they would like to come over for dinner on Sunday.

Increase the Positive Rewards of Sobriety

Next, review the positive consequences of drinking that you listed on your Decisional Matrix.

Despite the negative consequences of drinking, you have to remember that the positive consequences are what kept you drinking, and giving up those positive aspects of drinking is difficult. When people develop a drinking problem, they experience the "funneling effect": many resources—time, money, energy, attention—are directed toward alcohol, including thinking about alcohol, getting alcohol, drinking, being drunk, and recovering from alcohol's effects.

When people leave drinking behind, they often experience a frightening emptiness in their lives—the time and energy that drinking took has to be filled with something rewarding to keep you from going back to drinking. Try to think of it like this: One advantage of not drinking is that you have newfound freedom to use your time and resources in new ways, in whatever ways you choose. Let's make that a conscious choice. Let's think of ways to replace some of the positive consequences of drinking with rewarding activities that will be fun, positive, and healthy. To help you with that, review the list of activities that many people enjoy (Table 6.1).

Table 6.1 What Do Other People Do?

Read a book together	On a rainy day, clean the house together	Play games with your kids at the park
Put on music and dance together	Sort through old photos and start a scrapbook	Take a long walk on the boardwalk
Go out for a nice meal	Make funny faces at each other	Explore all the parks in your county
Do volunteer work	Go "treasure hunting" at garage sales on the weekends	Go to a free lecture at the local community college
Go to a county fair	Work backstage or build sets for your local community theater group	Do yard work together
Play cards or board games	Give each other massages	Take your dog to the park
Shop for new furniture for your home	Call an old friend who lives far away	Paint a room in your home
Begin a knitting or carpentry project	Go to a sporting event	Sign up for a cooking class or art course
Go to a concert or play	Go to a museum or art gallery	Visit the zoo or aquarium
Go on a picnic	Lounge by the pool, weather permitting	Go on a camping trip
Take a bike ride	Order in and watch a DVD	Go horseback riding
Buy different flavored donuts, taste them all, and rate them	Run errands together	Have a "sex" date
Take a dance or martial arts class	Go into the city and window shop	Pray together
Plant a vegetable garden	Catch fireflies	Take a shower or bath together
Plant flowers	Make dinner together	Plan a trip someplace new
Join a book club	Go rollerblading	Volunteer at your local place of worship

Alternatives to Drinking

Although some of the positive consequences of drinking (e.g., euphoria, relaxation) are not easily replaced, it is important to remember that they are artificial and temporary and usually followed by negative consequences.

Review the positive consequences of drinking that you listed on your Decisional Matrix and develop a list of positive, rewarding alternatives to drinking (e.g., relaxation, social activities, enjoying nature). Record alternatives on the worksheet on page 87. Be sure to select activities that fit with your long-term goals. For example, if one of your long-term goals is to get into better shape, you may wish to engage in physical activities like jogging or biking.

Alternatives to Drinking

Trigger situation and positive consequences of alcohol	Alternative activity with similar positive consequence
Some examples:	
Saturday night at restaurant with your spouse (positive consequences of alcohol: relaxation, wine goes with dinner, euphoria, festive atmosphere)	Get your favorite take-out food to eat at home and then go out to movie.
Tuesday night, spouse working late, and no one is home (positive consequences of alcohol: reduce loneliness, special time alone, relaxation)	Join a gym and go swimming Tuesday night, then stop on way home at Starbucks for decaf drink or browse the local bookstore.
Friday, after work, doing yard work (positive consequences of alcohol: relaxation)	Stop at gym to exercise on way home. Do the yard work Saturday morning instead.
Neighborhood picnic, Fourth of July (positive consequences of alcohol: more sociable, festive atmosphere, euphoria)	Go to gym before picnic, then bring your own soda. If too many tempting triggers at picnic, leave.

Shared Activities

In addition to choosing positive alternatives for yourself, you should also think of activities that you and your partner can share. This is yet another way to improve your relationship. Regardless of whatever else is going on, a couple can always come up with a block of 1–2 hours to do something pleasant together. All couples get stuck in routine ways of living together and feel there is nothing new or exciting to look forward to. Planning a new pleasurable, shared activity or reviving an old one and agreeing to be positive to each other can be satisfying. You both can agree to put aside everything else that's going on and do something that you both will find purely enjoyable.

Using the space provided, list activities you and your partner would like to share during the week. If you have difficulty thinking of activities, refer back to the list of what other people like to do.

Ideas for Enjoyable Activities

_____

_____

_____

_____

_____

_____

_____

_____

_____

Partners often try to protect the drinker from the consequences of drinking.

The result is that the drinker does not experience negative consequences that would help motivate him or her to quit. The protection helps maintain drinking. For example, you may shield the drinker from the embarrassment of having the children see him or her in a drunken condition. You may call your partner's boss and make excuses for absences. You may lie to family and friends to hide the drinking problems.

One common type of protection is to give comfort to the drinker who is suffering from the effects of a drinking episode. Many partners will care for the "sick" person. Instead of suffering the full consequences of the drinking, the drinker gets special attention.

Partners protect the drinker for many reasons. Out of love, they do not want the drinker to suffer. They also do not want the drinking to affect other family members, particularly children. In many situations, the partner wishes to protect the drinker's job because it is an important source of income for the family.

The partner who protects the problem drinker is denying the drinker a full and true knowledge of his or her own problem. When you protect the drinker, you are not giving these powerful negative consequences a chance to work. The protection unintentionally helps keep the drinking going.

You should agree together as a couple not to protect the drinker. If your partner has a future slip, you should refuse to do any special favors for him or her when he or she has been drinking. This means no hiding, making excuses, or caring for the sickly drinker. It was your partner's responsibility for drinking and it is also your partner's responsibility to cope with the consequences.

Make an agreement about what you will do if the drinker has a slip. The agreement should say that your partner is responsible for the consequences if he or she drinks. You should not try to make the consequences any easier.

Plan and practice for the possibility of a slip. Think of possible situations that may occur between you. Talk about how you will act.

You should imagine how you will handle the situation. Think of a likely situation. Go over in your imagination all the things that would happen. Imagine how you will firmly tell your partner that you will not make things easier. Rehearsing will make it easier to act at the right time.

Not protecting the drinker shows you care by getting your partner to face his or her drinking and the problems that result. Protecting your partner may lead to continued trouble.

Partner List of Protecting From Drinking

On this form, list all of your past "protection" behaviors. Write new, "non-protective" behaviors you can now do in each of these situations.

Protection	Alternative
Some examples:	
Calling your partner's boss when he or she is too drunk to go to work	Let your partner call
Bringing your partner food when he or she is in bed from drinking	Stay out of the room; eat without your partner
Your list:	

High-Risk Situations for the Week

Work with your therapist and partner to identify at least one high-risk situation coming up in the next week. Write down ideas about how to handle this situation on the High-Risk Situations worksheet. Use the back of your self-recording card to record how you actually handled the anticipated situation, and write down any unexpected high-risk situations that may have arisen during the week.

High-Risk Situations

What high-risk situations do you think you may experience this week?

Situation 1:

How can you handle this situation?

a.

_____

b.

_____

c.

_____

d.

_____

Situation 2:

How can you handle this situation?

a.

_____

b.

_____

c.

_____

d.

_____

Situation 3:

How can you handle this situation?

a.

_____

b.

_____

c.

_____

d.

_____

Situation 4:

How can you handle this situation?

a.

_____

b.

_____

c.

_____

d.

_____

Client Homework

✎ Continue self-recording. Remember to use the back of your self-recording cards to write down the ways you handled your high-risk situations for the week.

✎ Continue implementation of self-management plans. A blank copy of the Self-Management Planning Sheet is provided at the end of the chapter.

✎ Finish filling out the Alternatives to Drinking worksheet if not completed in session, and practice two alternatives this week.

✎ Hang negative consequences card where it is visible and read on a daily basis.

Partner Homework

✎ Continue recording your partner's alcohol use, urges (intensity), and your level of relationship satisfaction.

✎ Implement an alternative to one of your behaviors that is a trigger for your partner's drinking.

✎ Develop two more self-management plans. A blank copy of the Partner Self-Management Planning Sheet is provided at the end of the chapter.

✎ Make a list of new, non-protective reactions for each of the protection behaviors you identified earlier.

Couple Homework

✎ Review the information in this chapter.

✎ Have another urge discussion during the week.

✎ Carry out one shared pleasurable activity together.

Self-Management Planning Sheet

Trigger	Plan	+/−Consequences	Difficulty (1–10)
I.			
2.			

Partner Self-Management Planning Sheet

Trigger	Plan	+/−Consequences	Difficulty (1–10)
I.			
2.			

Chapter 7

Session 7: Dealing With Alcohol-Related Thoughts / Communication Part I

Goals

- To identify more activities that you and your partner can share over the next few weeks

- To learn to challenge and replace your dangerous thoughts about alcohol that lead to drinking

- To improve communication with your partner

Graphing Progress

As you have done every week, be sure to update your Alcohol Use and Urges and Relationship Satisfaction graphs in Chapter 2 using the information from your most recently completed self-recording cards.

Shared Activities Plan for Next Few Weeks

With your therapist, review the outcome of your first shared activity (refer to your list of enjoyable activities in the previous chapter). Then, identify shared activities for each of the next 2–3 weeks and list them in the space provided.

Planning for More Enjoyable Activities

_____

_____

_____

_____

_____

In this week's session, you will work with your therapist to restructure your thoughts about alcohol so they no longer serve as triggers for drinking.

Your thoughts lead to actions. People often do not realize how powerful their thoughts are. Sometimes these thoughts happen so quickly that people believe they are acting without thinking. If you could have an instant replay in slow motion, you could see how your thoughts lead to your actions.

Three types of thoughts can lead to drinking (see also Figure 7.1):

1. Thoughts about alcohol can create urges. Some examples are images of bars, thoughts about your favorite drink, and the smells and sounds of alcohol. These thoughts directly trigger urges.

2. Thoughts about the enjoyable effects of alcohol can trigger urges. Some examples are, "Just one won't hurt"; "It will calm my nerves"; "My friends will think I'm strange if I don't have a drink"; "It will help me sleep"; or "I can have just one." You probably listed some of these thoughts as positive consequences on your Decisional Matrix from Session 4. These thoughts are generally about the short-term benefits of drinking, and ignore the long-term problems it can cause.

3. Negative thinking can lead to drinking. Unpleasant thoughts and emotions can also lead to drinking. Some of these thoughts are about hopelessness or about negative self-worth. Examples are self-doubt, guilt, and anger. Negative thoughts are indirect triggers. They set up a chain of events that can lead to drinking.

What to Do?

The first step to stopping the drinking chains is to recognize the thoughts. You have already listed many of your own triggers (See Chapter 2). Among these triggers, you will find some dangerous thoughts.

Figure 7.1

Thoughts That Can Trigger Drinking

Remember the behavior chain (Refer back to Figure 2.1 in Chapter 2).

Your therapist will teach you the following two ways to manage your dangerous thoughts.

1. Identify and challenge dangerous thoughts about alcohol. When you have a positive thought about alcohol, once you recognize it you can *challenge* it. The challenge can be a reminder that the good things about alcohol lead to bad consequences, or you can question whether the positive thought about alcohol is even true. You then can *replace* the original positive thought with a more realistic one.

2. Think through the drink. When you think about drinking, keep thinking beyond the first desire to what will happen in the long run if you drink. In other words, think past the first drink to all that will follow.

Dealing With Alcohol-Related Thoughts

Use the worksheet on the next page to write down at least one personal example of each type of thought you have experienced that has led to drinking. Challenge each thought and come up with one that is more realistic and accurate.

Direct, Positive Thoughts About Alcohol: (for example, an image of a cold glass of beer)

_____

_____

Challenge and Replace:

_____

_____

2. Thoughts About Positive Consequences of Alcohol: (for example, "A glass of wine will taste good")

_____

_____

Challenge and Replace:

_____

_____

3. Negative Thinking: (for example, "I'm such a loser, I might as well drink too")

_____

_____

Challenge and Replace:

_____

_____

Communication Training

For the first several weeks, this program has focused on helping you stop drinking and teaching your partner how to respond to your drinking. Now, you will begin working together with your therapist to improve your communication skills.

To begin, think about the positive ways that you communicate with one another.

Strengths and Weaknesses in Our Communication

Using the worksheet provided, work together with your partner to list the positive aspects of the way you communicate with one another. You will list the negative aspects of your communication style later on in the session. For now, only complete the top half of the worksheet.

Strengths in our communication

_____

_____

_____

_____

_____

_____

_____

_____

_____

Weaknesses in our communication

_____

_____

_____

_____

_____

_____

_____

_____

Some Characteristics of Good Communication

The following are some good ways that couples can keep their lines of communication open:

- Be polite
  Show at least as much courtesy to your partner as you would to a stranger. Remember such simple things as saying "please" and "thank you" show you care about your partner's feelings.

- Listen carefully
  Too often we don't really listen to each other. Instead, when the other person is talking we are preparing our return argument or thinking about what we want to say next. Listening doesn't mean you agree, but it does mean that you care enough about your partner's opinions and feelings to really hear what they are.

- Validate your partner
  If you really listen, you may understand more about your partner's feelings or ideas. Validating means telling your partner that you do understand or that he or she has a very good point. It doesn't mean that you agree, only that you can understand your partner's point of view.

- Tell your partner about the good feelings you have
  Let your partner know, with words and actions, exactly what he or she does to make you feel good. Many people wrongly assume that their partner will just know these things. Expressing your feelings reminds your partner that he or she is important.

- Do favors for your partner
  The small things you do for one another add up. We know that couples who do many small things for one another have fewer difficulties handling disagreements. Think of it as investing in your relationship.

- Stop and think before commenting on something irritating
  Ask yourself if the issue is really important. Decide if the consequences of bringing up something minor are worth it.

- Choose the right place and time to bring up a problem
Talk about your worries, concerns, or irritations when other things will not distract you. Choose a time when both of you can devote your energies to the problem.

- Have a goal for every complaint
Complaining for the sake of complaining does not accomplish much. Think of your complaint as a problem that you and your partner should solve together. When you have a complaint, think of a specific thing that you would like to change.

- If you have a complaint, stick to one thing at a time
We have a term for piling on many complaints at once. We call it "kitchen sinking." Instead of kitchen sinking, focus on one problem at a time. Bringing up many things at once will be overwhelming and may sound like blaming.

- Ask for change in a positive manner
Describe what your partner can do differently and how it will make you happier. Avoid being critical.

- Expect to compromise
There are two ways to compromise:

  1. Each of you gets a part of what you want and gives up a little of something.
  2. One of you gets what you want now, but in exchange, the other person may get his or her way in another situation.

At first, some of these things will be difficult. As a couple, you have developed many habits that will need to change. Often, couples get stuck because no one wants to be the first to do something positive. Remember that each of you is totally responsible for your own actions—you can do these things despite what your partner does. The benefits begin when someone (you) takes the first step.

Signs of Bad Communication

Refer back to the worksheet where you listed the strengths of your communication. Now, go back and list some of the weaknesses you may experience when trying to communicate with one another.

Every couple needs to work to have good communication. Following are some traps into which couples fall.

- Not listening
  Listening is a complicated job. You must hear what is said, figure out what was intended, check if you understand by getting feedback, and validate what the other person is saying.

- Mind reading
  People often assume they know what is on the other person's mind. This is a dangerous trap. The assumptions are often wrong and lead to trouble. Even if you have known someone for a long time, you cannot know for sure what your partner is thinking. Always check with your partner to make sure you understand what he or she is thinking.

- Yes-butting
  Yes-butting is when the listener does not really listen but keeps talking about what is on his or her mind. In this kind of bad communication, the listener will say, "Yes, but ...." Listen and communicate to your partner that you are taking what he or she says seriously. Repeat it back to him or her in your own words.

- Drifting off topic
  Many couples will start an important conversation but end up talking about things not related to the main issue. By drifting around the subject, couples do not resolve important problems. When discussing a problem, stick to one issue at a time.

- Interrupting
  Interrupting is not only rude it also keeps the listener from ever hearing what the other person has to say. Wait until the other person finishes before speaking.

- Standoff routine
  Couples get into a routine of arguing and then waiting for the other person to back down. Nobody backs down because he or she would see this as losing face. Accept responsibility! Be willing to take the first steps toward making up.

- Heavy silence or escalating quarrels
  Two symptoms of bad communication are silent treatments and arguments that constantly get out of control. Use assertive communication skills to discuss a problem with your partner.

- Never stopping the action to get feedback

  Another symptom is for couples in arguments to keep going and not trying to figure out why the conversation is going so badly. This problem communication means that arguments go in circles without the partners understanding one another. When arguments seem like they are going in circles, stop and ask your partner what he or she is feeling or thinking. You can then solve the misunderstandings that create bad communication.

- Insulting and personally attacking each other

  Insults and personal attacks just make the other person angrier. Insults make arguments and relationships worse, never better. Honey is better than vinegar when dealing with loved ones.

- Not valuing what the other person says

  People who put down what other people say cannot have healthy communication. Statements like "that is ridiculous" or "that is stupid" not only put down the other person they also signal poor listening. Always show respect for what your partner says.

- Kitchen sinking

  As mentioned earlier, kitchen sinking happens when people bring old problems into a disagreement. The disagreement sounds like a laundry list of complaints instead of healthy problem solving. To the partner, the laundry list sounds like an attack coming from many sides. He or she will usually get defensive. Stick to one issue at a time when discussing a problem.

- Character assassination

  Much like insults, character assassination shows disrespect. Instead of focusing on the problem, a person talks about what is wrong with the other person. Angry partners will attack each other instead of focusing on fixing the problem. Stick to discussing the problem at hand.

High-Risk Situations for the Week

Work with your therapist and partner to identify at least one high-risk situation coming up in the next week. Write down ideas about how to handle this situation on the High-Risk Situations worksheet. Use the back of your self-recording card to record how you actually handled the anticipated situation, and write down any unexpected high-risk situations that may have arisen during the week.

High-Risk Situations

What high-risk situations do you think you may experience this week?

Situation 1:

How can you handle this situation?

a.

b.

c.

d.

Situation 2:

How can you handle this situation?

a.

b.

c.

d.

Situation 3:

How can you handle this situation?

a.

b.

c.

d.

Situation 4:

How can you handle this situation?

a.

b.

c.

d.

Client Homework

✎ Continue self-recording. Remember to use the back of your self-recording cards to write down the ways you handled your high-risk situations for the week.

✎ Continue to refer to your negative consequences card from Chapter 6 whenever you are faced with high-risk situations.

✎ Start to develop a new thinking habit—finish filling out the Dealing With Alcohol-Related Thoughts worksheet.

Partner Homework

✎ Continue recording your partner's alcohol use, urges (intensity), and your level of relationship satisfaction.

✎ Implement two more trigger alternatives this week.

✎ Select and practice one non-protection scenario during the week.

Couple Homework

✎ Review the information in this chapter.

✎ Carry out a shared pleasurable activity.

Chapter 8

Session 8: Drink Refusal / Communication Part II

Goals

- To practice drink refusal skills
- To learn the five steps of good communication

Graphing Progress

As you have done every week, be sure to update your Alcohol Use and Urges and Relationship Satisfaction graphs in Chapter 2 using the information from your most recently completed self-recording cards.

Extending the Shared Activity

This week, work with your partner to refine your shared activity. In the space provided, each of you should list three behaviors that you would like to see your partner do more of during the fun activity. For example, if you agree to go out to dinner, one of you may want your partner to hold your hand or give you a compliment or hang up your coat. The overall intent is to increase the positive experiences you have with each other.

Client—Things I want my partner to increase:

_____

_____

_____

Partner—Things I want my partner to increase:

_____

_____

_____

The ability to refuse drinks is much more difficult than it appears. It is another weapon in your arsenal of skills to stay sober. In the session, you are going to practice ways of refusing/turning down drinks so that you can gain control in these tough situations.

One-third of problem drinkers have a slip because of pressure from others. Refusing offers of drinks is harder than most people think. It takes special skills to say no to drinks.

Offers of drinks come in many forms. Sometimes friends or co-workers put pressure on you to join in their drinking. Other times the pressure comes from family members. Sometimes you may be concerned about what others will think if you refuse the drink.

Some people are easier to refuse than others. Some will politely accept your first refusal. Others may get pushy.

Drink refusal is an important assertiveness skill. The foundation of assertiveness skills is respect for your own needs. Remember that individuals who encourage you to drink are pushers and must be discouraged politely but firmly. Be firm without getting aggressive. By using the following skills, you can refuse a drink without coming on too strong.

How to refuse drinks:

- No should be the first thing you say. Starting with no makes it tougher for the pusher to try to manipulate you.

- Look the person in the eye when you speak. Eye contact makes you come across as firm. Not looking the other person in the eye tells him or her that you are not sure about what you are saying.

- Speak clearly and in a serious tone. Your manner should say that you mean business.

- You have a right to say no. You want to stay sober. It is your life that you are protecting. Do not feel guilty.

- Suggest alternatives. If someone is offering a drink, ask for something non-alcoholic. If someone is asking you to get into a risky situation, suggest something else that is not risky.

- Change the subject to a new topic of conversation. Get the pusher to think about something else.

- Ask the person not to continue offering you a drink. Someone who is pushing you to drink is not respecting your rights. Ask him or her to leave you alone.

- Know your bottom line. You are saying no out of respect for yourself. If the person keeps pushing, use your problem solving skills. Remember, you can leave, get the person to leave, or get help from others.

- And finally . . . Practice, practice, practice!

These skills are difficult to use in a real-life situation. Social pressure is one of the most difficult problems that people face. Many people you know drink or expect you to drink. They will have a difficult time accepting the change.

Think of different situations you may face. Develop some strategies for handling each. Practice with your therapist how you would use these skills. Practice at home—use the mirror. Practice in real situations when you feel ready. Remember to reward yourself for doing the right thing!

Drink Refusal Examples

You're at your brother's house on Christmas Day. It's a special occasion; you are with family and friends. Your brother says, "How about a beer?" You say, "No thanks, I'd like a soda though."

A group of your friends stop by your house or approach you at a party and offer you a drink. They say, "Hey Jill, how about a glass of wine?" You say, "No thanks, I'm not drinking." They say, "Oh come on! One drink won't hurt. What kind of friend are you?" or "What's the matter? Are you too good to drink with us?" You say, "I'll just take a mineral water with lime, thanks."

Good Communication

After practicing your drink refusal skills, you therapist will introduce you to the model of good communication.

Many disagreements start when one person misunderstands what the other person is saying. Many things can happen to create misunderstandings.

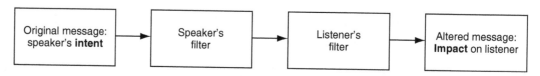

Figure 8.1

Communication Filters

Communication is a very complicated thing that we take for granted. One partner may wish to say something. We call this the *intent*. The other partner may understand something completely different from what the first partner wished to say. This is called the *impact* of the statement. Many things get between the intent and the impact of a message. Some of these things are called filters. Filters change a message to be something different from what the speaker intended. Both the speaker and the listener have filters that change a message (see Figure 8.1).

Notice what happens in the following situation:

> *John has had a hard day at work. He was up against a deadline, and his boss was in his office and emailing him every half hour. He's very tired, but he and Rachel are going out to dinner with a woman Rachel knew from high school, and her husband. Rachel is very tense about the dinner—she wants to look good because this woman was very popular and pretty and Rachel had felt a little inferior to her when they were in high school. John is tired and distracted and is still worrying that he might have overlooked something in the project, but doesn't say anything to Rachel because he doesn't want to ruin the evening by focusing on work.*

Rachel (Wanting reassurance that she looks good): Do these pants look okay on me?

John (Always thinks she looks great and doesn't realize that she's insecure, is still worrying about work): Yeah, they're fine.

Rachel (Thinks he's saying she looks bad): Do you think I should change?

John (Still distracted): No, you're fine.

Rachel (Now she is convinced that she looks terrible and that John is half-ignoring her because he doesn't want to go out): Look, I don't care if you don't want to go out; this is important to me. I want to look good, and I want you to be on your best behavior too.

John (Totally confused that she's upset):   I don't understand why you're so worked up about this—it's only dinner with an old friend, and you look good—you always look good.

Rachel (Angry):   Don't patronize me. I hate it when you do that!

Notice that John's intent was to compliment Rachel, but because of his own distraction and bad mood, he didn't sound complimentary. Rachel didn't know he was upset, so she tried to guess what he was thinking. She guessed wrong, but never realized it.

Good communication means having the impact you intended to have. That is, intent equals impact. Good communication between partners is clear and specific. The speaker tries to clarify the intent of his or her message by stating exactly what he or she is thinking, wanting, or feeling. He or she does not assume the listener can mind-read. The good listener tries to make sure that he or she understands the intent of the message. He or she does not try to guess at meanings.

Misunderstandings often happen. Sometimes they lead to funny stories. Other times they poison the relationship. You will have a better relationship if you understand that communication can be very complicated. There are many ways for things to go wrong. In John and Rachel's example, they were tired and nervous about the evening. Their emotional and physical condition affected how they heard each other. They probably have some history of misunderstandings that contributed to this problem. Both John and Rachel had filters that affected their communication. Filters change a message from what they intend to what they hear. The following are some examples of filters that affect the speaker and the listener (see Table 8.1). Notice that the filters are similar for both of them.

Table 8.1 Speaker and Listener Filters

Speaker filters	Listener filters
Not saying what we really mean. In the example, the speakers were not clear in speaking what was on their mind.	Often we do not listen because we are thinking about a response. Not paying attention leads to the person ignoring everything the speaker says.
Leaving out information or assuming the listener already knows something. We often expect the listener to know why we are saying something. The problem is that listeners are not mind-readers.	Making assumptions based on too little information. The listeners in our story assumed that there were hidden reasons behind what the speaker said.

continued

Table 8.1 Speaker and Listener Filters *continued*

Speaker filters	Listener filters
Moods often affect the way we say something. In this example, Rachel might have said things differently if she had not been so tense. Moods affect how we say things.	Moods affect how we interpret what someone else says. If we are in a happy mood, we will hear something as funny. If we are tired and worried, we may hear the same words as threatening.
The history of problems in the relationship may affect our communication. If things our partner has done irritate us, we will not put the same care into saying something. Many couples bring unrelated problems into a disagreement.	The history of problems in the relationship may affect how we hear what our partner says. Old problems influence how we interpret what the other person is saying. We may suspect they connect the current statement to the old problem.

Here are five steps to take when you are feeling misunderstood:

1. Call a stop action: You stop the discussion so you can talk about what's happening.

2. Feedback: Ask for feedback—what did the listener think you said? When giving feedback, make it clear, brief, specific, and on topic. You are giving information to make things better, not trying to get even.

3. Listen to feedback: What is the content? What is the feeling?

4. Summarize and validate: Summarize the content of what was said and your partner's feelings. Try to get into your partner's shoes to understand why your partner feels this way. Communicate your understanding of your partner's feelings—if you were seeing things his or her way, it would make sense to feel that way. Saying you understand your partner's feelings does not mean you agree, only that you are listening and trying to understand. This is very hard to do, especially when you yourself feel hurt or not listened to.

5. Check impact: Check your impact compared to your intent, and try to explain again.

High-Risk Situations for the Week

Work with your therapist and partner to identify at least one high-risk situation coming up in the next week. Write down ideas about how to handle this situation on the High-Risk Situations worksheet. Use the back of your self-recording card to record how you actually handled the anticipated situation, and write down any unexpected high-risk situations that may have arisen during the week.

High-Risk Situations

What high-risk situations do you think you may experience this week?

Situation 1:

How can you handle this situation?

a.

_____

b.

_____

c.

_____

d.

_____

Situation 2:

How can you handle this situation?

a.

_____

b.

_____

c.

_____

d.

_____

Situation 3:

How can you handle this situation?

a.

_____

b.

_____

c.

_____

d.

_____

Situation 4:

How can you handle this situation?

a.

_____

b.

_____

c.

_____

d.

_____

Homework

Client Homework

✎ Continue self-recording. Remember to use the back of your self-recording cards to write down the ways you handled your high-risk situations for the week.

✎ Determine a situation during the next week in which you will be offered alcohol. Practice your refusal scenes twice daily.

✎ Continue employing self-control procedures.

Partner Homework

✎ Continue recording your partner's alcohol use, urges (intensity), and your level of relationship satisfaction.

Couple Homework

✎ Review the information in this chapter.

✎ Participate in a shared activity and be sure to incorporate the three new behaviors you each requested of one another.

✎ Have a discussion of a topic around which you have mild disagreement, to practice the 5-step good communication technique practiced in session.

Chapter 9

Session 9: Partner Role in Drink Refusal / Communication Part III / Relapse Prevention Part I

Goals

- For your partner to learn what he or she can do to help you in typical drink-refusal situations

- To learn how to handle conflict within your relationship

- To start learning about relapses and how to avoid them by discussing the impact of seemingly irrelevant decisions on your drinking

Graphing Progress

As you have done every week, be sure to update your Alcohol Use and Urges and Relationship Satisfaction graphs in Chapter 2 using the information from your most recently completed self-recording cards.

For the Partner—How Can I Help When Alcohol Is Present?

As a couple, you may be together in many situations where alcohol is present. When this happens, it is important to remember the following:

- It is the drinker's responsibility to decide not to drink, but as the partner, you can help.

- You may make it easier for your partner to stay sober and you'll feel better knowing what you can do to help.

- The key is to talk ahead of time about what you can do.

Here's an example.

Leonard and Suzanne had some friends over for dinner. Leonard usually is generous with drinks, but didn't offer them any alcohol:

Suzanne: You usually give Harold and Maude drinks, why didn't you tonight?

Leonard: Because I was helping you stay sober.

Suzanne: Well that makes me mad because I feel like a baby. Why should others be deprived because of me? I felt so embarrassed!

Leonard: Well I was only helping since you've been off it such a short time.

Suzanne: You are patronizing me. I am getting mad.

Leonard: No I am not; I am helping you, dear!

Suzanne: Well that kind of help I don't need! You don't understand me at all!

Leonard thought he was helping, but without talking to Suzanne first, he made the situation worse. He could have asked Suzanne ahead of time:

Leonard: Harold and Maude are coming over tonight. I usually offer them drinks before dinner. I wonder what you think would be most helpful for you tonight.

Suzanne: I don't want them to feel deprived. Seeing them drink won't give me an urge.

Suzanne also could have looked ahead and talked with Leonard:

Suzanne: Harold and Maude are coming over tonight. It's okay with me if you serve them drinks, but don't ask me what I want—just give me a seltzer with a twist, and don't say anything about my not drinking. I'm not ready to tell them yet.

There are lots of ways to help:

- Offer to get your partner a non-alcoholic drink so he or she doesn't have to go to the bar.

- Order the non-alcoholic drink of your partner's choice in a restaurant, or say nothing so that your partner can order him or herself.

- Give your partner a warm look, or touch your partner for a moment to let him or her know you're thinking about him or her in a drinking situation.

- Be willing to leave a social event early if your partner's just having too hard a time.

- Join the conversation if you think someone is pushing your partner too hard and he or she is getting frustrated.

- Keep in mind that your partner hasn't been sober that long and that any situation with alcohol present may be a challenge.

Remember—there are no right answers—just be sure that you know how your partner wants you to help.

When Alcohol Is Present

Use the following worksheet to list ways that you can help your partner when he or she is faced with a high-risk situation.

Situation: _____

What I could do:

_____

_____

_____

Situation: _____

What I could do:

_____

_____

_____

Situation: _____

What I could do:

_____

_____

_____

Situation: _____

What I could do:

_____

_____

_____

In this session, your therapist will talk to you about direct and assertive communication, building on the information from the previous two sessions.

Two types of conflict create trouble for couples: constant bickering and avoidance. With bickering, the couple constantly fights or argues without resolving anything. In avoidance, the partners never bring up anything that could lead to an argument. Both types of conflict patterns are bad for the relationship.

The most obvious pattern of conflict that occurs in relationships is arguing or fighting. Research shows that people are more polite to strangers than to their partners. Many couples get themselves into a pattern of saying anything they may be thinking. They do not stop to consider whether it is insulting or senseless. They interrupt their partners more, put their partners down more, hurt each other's feelings more, and are less complimentary to each other.

For this type of fighting, the partners need more politeness and editing. To break this pattern, the individuals need to stop and think about the importance and damage caused by what they will say. Everyone must learn how to edit out unimportant or insulting things that will poison communication. Partners must realize that they cannot say everything that is on their mind. As previously discussed, our thoughts are not always healthy.

The second pattern of couple conflict is avoidance. Avoidance happens when one partner gives in most of the time, or both partners quietly ignore a problem issue. Although the couple never seems to disagree, they are in conflict as someone usually feels resentful or unappreciated. Some issues are important and need to be discussed.

The way to break out of both patterns is to:

- Become more aware of your own feelings—what makes you feel good and what makes you feel unhappy.

- Level with your partner about what he or she does that makes you unhappy. Tell your partner what he or she can do to change the situation. A constructive way to level is to use statements like the following: "I feel X, when you do Y, in situation Z."

Some examples of X-Y-Z statements are as follows:

- "I feel stressed and hassled when you ask me for things when we first get up in the morning."

- "I feel lonely and embarrassed when you don't introduce me to people at a party and don't spend time with me."

- "I feel hurt when you criticize my driving."

- "I feel angry when you spend money on things that are not within our budget."

Expressing your feelings directly and respectfully is the key to being heard and solving problems.

X, Y, Z Worksheet

Work with your partner to develop some X-Y-Z statements for 5 simple issues. Write them down here.

1. _____

_____

_____

2. _____

_____

_____

3. _____

_____

_____

4. _____

_____

_____

5. _____

_____

_____

Many of the ordinary choices that you make every day seem to have nothing to do with drinking. Although these choices do not appear to be related to drinking, often you will find that small decisions lead to trigger situations. This is the domino effect of small decisions. One decision leads to another, which leads to another, and so on. A number of small decisions may bring you closer to a high-risk situation. Put together, the decisions that set up drinking are what we call "seemingly irrelevant decisions."

Think about this story:

Jeff is on his way home from work and hasn't had a drink in 5 months. He's gotten to the point where he catches himself not thinking about alcohol for 2 to 3 days at a time. It's hot outside and he wants to get home, but today there's a 10 million dollar lottery and he wants to stop to buy a couple of lottery tickets. He pulls into the liquor store/bar he used to frequent; he knows they sell lottery tickets there. He buys the tickets and is about to turn around and walk out when he hears his name being called. He looks behind him and sees Rich, an old drinking buddy, waving him over to the bar. He walks over to say hi, and finds an ice-cold beer that Rich has ordered for him, waiting at the counter. Before he can stop himself, he downs the beer and orders another.

You may be able to see that Jeff made a series of decisions that led to his final decision to drink. For each one of the choices, Jeff could have made a different decision that would have led him away from a risky situation. Did he really need to buy his lottery ticket at a bar? Did he have to walk over to his old drinking buddy, or could he have just waved hello to him? Could he have said "no" to himself about the first beer? Jeff made a series of decisions. Each one of the decisions contributed to his finally drinking.

People often think of themselves as victims: "Things just seemed to happen in such a way that I ended up in a high-risk situation and then had a drink—I could not help it." They think things happen to them without realizing that many little decisions get them into trouble. That is because many of the decisions do not actually seem to involve drinking. Each choice you make may take you just a little closer to drinking. When alcohol is not on your mind, you will find it more difficult to make the connection between a choice and later trouble.

The best solution is to think about the choices you make. By thinking ahead about each possible option, you can look ahead for possible trouble. In the beginning, you may find thinking about every decision to be awkward. Eventually, you will find it easier to do. With practice, you will find that you think about potential trouble automatically.

By paying more attention to each decision, you will stop the chain of events that leads to drinking. It is much easier to stop the process early rather than later when you are in the middle of a high-risk situation. When you have a decision to make, choose a low-risk option. If you have to make a high-risk decision, plan ahead to protect yourself.

High-Risk Situations for the Week

Work with your therapist and partner to identify at least one high-risk situation coming up in the next week. Write down ideas about how to handle this situation on the High-Risk Situations worksheet. Use the back of your self-recording card to record how you actually handled the anticipated situation, and write down any unexpected high-risk situations that may have arisen during the week.

High-Risk Situations

What high-risk situations do you think you may experience this week?

Situation 1:

How can you handle this situation?

a.

_____

b.

_____

c.

_____

d.

_____

Situation 2:

How can you handle this situation?

a.

_____

b.

_____

c.

_____

d.

_____

Situation 3:

How can you handle this situation?

a.

_____

b.

_____

c.

_____

d.

_____

Situation 4:

How can you handle this situation?

a.

_____

b.

_____

c.

_____

Homework

Client Homework

✎ Continue self-recording. Remember to use the back of your self-recording cards to write down the ways you handled your high-risk situations for the week.

✎ Think about a decision you have made recently or are about to make. The decision could involve any aspect of your life, such as your job, recreational activities, friends, or family. Identify safe choices that might decrease your risk for relapse, and record these on the Seemingly Irrelevant Decisions worksheet at the end of the chapter.

Partner Homework

✎ Continue recording your partner's alcohol use, urges (intensity), and your level of relationship satisfaction.

Couple Homework

✎ Review the information in this chapter.

✎ Decide together how to handle two more drink refusal situations.

✎ Role-play at home or practice in a real situation the partner's role in drink refusal.

✎ Discuss another topic at home, selecting one at a moderate level of disagreement, using the good communication skills you learned, incorporating X, Y, Z feedback as needed.

Seemingly Irrelevant Decisions

Safe Choices   **Risky Choices**

_____   _____

_____   _____

_____   _____

_____   _____

_____   _____

_____   _____

_____   _____

_____   _____

_____   _____

_____   _____

_____   _____

_____   _____

_____   _____

_____   _____

_____   _____

_____   _____

_____   _____

Chapter 10

Session 10: Problem Solving / Relapse Prevention Part II

Goals

- To learn how to problem solve effectively

- To identify warning signs for relapse and devise plans for handling them when they come up

Graphing Progress

As you have done every week, be sure to update your Alcohol Use and Urges and Relationship Satisfaction graphs in Chapter 2 using the information from your most recently completed self-recording cards.

Problem Solving

In this session, you will learn about problem solving and how to use it as a general coping skill.

Everyone has faced a big problem that seemed impossible to conquer. Some people get lost in the problem and do not find a solution. Other people go through a method that helps them solve it.

There is a method that many people use to solve difficult problems. This method is easy to understand. You will need to go through a number of steps to solve a problem. As with any new skill, you will need to practice using this method to solve problems. The more you use it, the easier it gets. At first, you will find the method a little awkward. But the more you use it, the more natural it will seem to you.

The skills presented here can be applied to any part of your life. You have already used some of these skills when you talked about coping with urges and planning for difficult situations.

The problem-solving method has seven steps:

1. Gather information: Think about the problem situation. Who is involved? When does it happen? Exactly what takes place? What effect does this have on you? What happens before the problem (the antecedents)? What keeps the problem going (the consequences)? Where does it occur? How does the problem affect you?

2. Define the problem: What is the goal that you would like to achieve? Be clear and specific. Many people get into trouble at this step because they select very vague goals. Define your goal as something that can be counted. The more specific and real you make the problem, the easier it will be to solve.

3. Brainstorm for alternatives: This can be a fun step. The goal of this step is to build a long list of possible solutions. The first rule of brainstorming is that no idea is too silly or dumb. Try to think about any and every possible solution to the problem. Do not think about how good or bad each idea is—that will come later. By not evaluating the ideas as they come, you will be more creative in thinking of solutions. Make as long a list as you can. The number of ideas is more important than their quality.

4. Now, consider the consequences of each: For each of your alternatives, list the positive and negative consequences. Think about the short-term and long-term results of each solution. Ask yourself: What things can you reasonably expect to happen? What will be the positive consequences? What will be the negative consequences? Which consequences will happen right away? Which consequences will happen later? How can you combine different alternatives?

5. Decide: Which of the alternatives is the most likely to achieve the goal you set in Step 2? Look for the solution (or solutions) that have the best balance of consequences.

6. Do it! The best plan in the world is useless if you do not put it into action. Try it out.

7. Evaluate: Check out how the plan is working. Which parts work best? Which parts can you improve? Fix what can be fixed.

Reward yourself for taking action! You have done something to help yourself.

Problem-Solving Example

1. Problem definition:

   - Background: Susan and Steven live together and often find themselves arguing about division of labor around the house. From Steven's perspective, he does far more around the house than Susan, and he feels resentful toward her.
   - Specific problem situation: Steven wants to find a different way to deal with this situation so he feels that the division of labor is more fair.

2. Brainstorming for alternatives:

   - Keep trying to ask Susan to do tasks around the house.
   - Stop asking Susan and just do all the tasks himself.
   - Hire a housecleaner and a landscape company.
   - Stop doing his share of the chores and tasks around the house.
   - Tell Susan he thinks they need to go to marital therapy to work out these issues.

3. Decision making (choosing the most effective alternative):

Evaluate the positive and negative consequences of each possible alternative.

Choose the alternative with the best payoff, solving the problem while maximizing positive consequences and minimizing negatives.

Solution	Pros (short and long term)	Cons (short and long term)
Steven could keep trying to get Susan to help around the house	It's what he's been doing anyway	It hasn't been working Steven may end up feeling resentful
Steven could simply stop asking Susan to help	This would avoid confrontation	Steven may end up resenting Susan even more
Steven could hire a housekeeper	This would reduce chores and tasks There would be less for Steven and Susan to argue over	A housekeeper is expensive Steven would still resent Susan for not helping with chores

continued

continued

Solution	Pros (short and long term)	Cons (short and long term)
Steven could stop doing his chores and tasks	This would give him more time to relax It may force Susan to take over some of the responsibilities	The house may end up getting dirty and staying that way More resentment The bills may be late It's a passive-aggressive solution
Steven could tell Susan he wants to go to marital therapy	This would give the couple a chance to discuss issues without arguing	Therapy is expensive Therapy is time consuming Susan may get angry and might not want to go

Problem-Solving Worksheet

Pick a problem that has come up in the course of treatment so far and practice solving it using the methods just described.

1. Gather Information: _____

2. Problem Definition: _____

3. Brainstorming for Solutions and Listing of Pros and Cons:

Solution	Pros (short and long term)	Cons (short and long term)
a.		
b.		
c.		
d.		
e.		

4. Pick solution(s): _____

5. Implement the solution for a period of time.

6. Reevaluate the solution—Did it work? _____

If not, do problem solving again.

Now, you will talk about how problem solving can work for you and your partner together. It's important that you set aside time each week to talk about issues and concerns. Having a set "family meeting" time can make it easier to deal with problems.

Constant complaining without solutions is a sign of bad communication. Gripes are complaints about small or less important irritations that create conflict. You should not bring up every gripe since this may lead to bickering. One way to talk about these gripes in a healthy way is the family meeting. The family meeting is an opportunity for you and other family members to come together to solve problems. The family meeting is a special time for working on the things that create conflict. Family meetings can be scheduled one or two times a week at a specific time. It is a time to use good communication skills. A family meeting has three stages:

1. Gripe time

2. Agenda building

3. Problem solving

Gripe Time

Gripe time is an opportunity to communicate concerns, irritations, and disappointments. Gripes should be stated using X, Y, Z statements. The listener should not become defensive. He or she should work hard at understanding what is said and having empathy (put yourself in your partner's shoes). Everyone should follow the list of do's and don'ts:

Do's	Dont's
Do state clearly and specifically the gripes you have about your partner	Don't try to defend yourself by showing that your partner is wrong
Do follow the rules for constructive leveling	Don't sulk and withdraw when you gripe
Do listen and accept your partner's gripes as legitimate feelings	Don't meet your partner's gripe with a gripe of your own. Don't cross-complain. Don't assume you know what your partner means; make sure

Partners should help each other get specific about gripes. Ask:

- What specifically did I do that bothered you?

- In what situations (when and where)?

- Can you give me examples?

- Can you point out the problem the next time it happens?

Agenda Building

During this part of the meeting, the couple decides what specific issues they want to work on during the meeting. Pick one major issue. Do not throw in new gripes. Use all the good communication skills.

Define the problem in a clear and specific way. Following is a list of some of the features of good and bad problem definitions.

Good problem definitions:

- are mutually agreed upon

- outline each partner's role in the problem

- include a simple and specific description of the problem

- include a description of each partner's feelings

- include something positive

Bad problem definitions:

- state only one partner's view

- are accusatory and blaming

- tend to be general and vague

- list each person's gripes about the problem

- focus only on the negative

Problem Solving

Gripe time turns general comments into specific concerns. Agenda building helps define the problems and set priorities. During agenda building, the couple picks one issue to work on. Problem solving is the time dedicated to building solutions. Review the problem-solving procedure for working on the problem and focus on finding solutions. Once you are done with brainstorming, discuss the pros and cons of the best alternatives. Normally, couples make an agreement about increasing a specific positive behavior. They spell out the specific times, situations, and responsibilities for the behavior change. The most successful meetings end with everyone agreeing on a specific solution. The solution spells out the details of what should and should not be done.

Family Meeting Worksheet

Gripe Time—what do we have on our minds?

_____

_____

Agenda Building—what is the one problem we should discuss today?

_____

Problem Solving:

1. Gather Information: _____

2. Problem Definition: _____

3. Brainstorming for Solutions and Listing of Pros and Cons:

Solution	Pros (short and long term)	Cons (short and long term)
a.		
b.		
c.		
d.		
e.		

4. Pick solution(s): _____

5. Implement the solution for a period of time.

6. Reevaluate the solution—Did it work? _____

If not, do problem solving again.

Until now, we have talked about remaining abstinent from alcohol. The goal is for you to stop drinking completely. We have focused on skills that help you remain abstinent in the long run. However, we do know that many people who want to stay sober may have difficulties from time to time. The best skill is to be aware of warning signs and handle them without drinking. However, people do have slips, and while we do not want this to happen, we believe it is important to be ready for possible slips.

We want you to think about warning signs of relapse. It may seem pessimistic to discuss drinking, but we like to think about relapse prevention the way we think about fire prevention. For fire prevention, we look at possible dangers in our homes, schools, and workplaces. We know where the fire extinguishers are and how to contact the fire department. We remain aware of possible trouble: something flammable near a heat source or strange smoke. Similarly, we should remain aware of signs of trouble about possible drinking.

Warning signs might be changes in the way either of you think and interact, or changes in habits. You have learned many new behaviors. Through dedication, these behaviors can become everyday habits. Changes in these new habits may signal trouble. Look out for old habits, especially ones that led to trouble in the past. Look for changes in mood, people you associate with, places you go to, ways you handle problems, and routines. Be alert for changes in the way you think about alcohol, yourself, or things around you. All these things could signal the possibility of a slip.

Think back to your last slip. What were the signals of trouble? Remember the few days before the slip. What things had changed? Look for changes in actions or thoughts that may have warned you of trouble. These old signals are ones you should watch for.

Use the following worksheet to list the thoughts, feelings, and behaviors that you experienced before your last lapse. These are your warning signs. You will talk about how to handle these warning signs later on in the session.

Identifying and Managing Relapse Warning Signs

Drinker's warning signs

How to handle warning signs

1. _____

1. _____

_____

_____

2. _____

2. _____

_____

_____

3. _____

3. _____

_____

_____

4. _____

4. _____

_____

_____

5. _____

5. _____

_____

_____

Think about any changes in your partner's behavior or mood during the same period of time before your latest relapse. Did your partner engage in counterproductive behaviors such as threatening or discussing past drinking? Did your partner act controlling in a drinking situation? Did your partner change any of his or her habits, moods, or people he or she was spending time with? Work together with your partner to list his or her warning signs on the worksheet provided.

Partner's warning signs

1. _____

_____

2. _____

_____

3. _____

_____

4. _____

_____

5. _____

_____

How to handle warning signs

1. _____

_____

2. _____

_____

3. _____

_____

4. _____

_____

5. _____

_____

Next, think about any ways that your interactions were different, in terms of arguments, the quality of your time together, or how you were handling problems. List your shared warning signs on the following worksheet.

Couple's warning signs:

1. _____

_____

2. _____

_____

3. _____

_____

4. _____

_____

5. _____

_____

How to handle warning signs:

1. _____

_____

2. _____

_____

3. _____

_____

4. _____

_____

5. _____

_____

Managing Warning Signs for Relapse

Your therapist is going to help you prepare to face situations that will occur after treatment ends. Having a list of warning signs for relapses does not necessarily mean that you will be aware of them as warning signs when they actually occur—remember the discussion of seemingly irrelevant decisions from Chapter 9?

Review the relapse warning signs that you and your partner listed on the preceding worksheets, and discuss a *plan* for what to do if any of the signs should occur. Write down the plans in the spaces provided on the worksheets.

High-Risk Situations for the Week

Work with your therapist and partner to identify at least one high-risk situation coming up in the next week. Write down ideas about how to handle this situation on the High-Risk Situations worksheet. Use the back of your self-recording card to record how you actually handled the anticipated situation, and write down any unexpected high-risk situations that may have arisen during the week.

High-Risk Situations

What high-risk situations do you think you may experience this week?

Situation 1:

How can you handle this situation?

a.

_____

b.

_____

c.

_____

d.

_____

Situation 2:

How can you handle this situation?

a.

_____

b.

_____

c.

_____

d.

_____

Situation 3:

How can you handle this situation?

a.

_____

b.

_____

c.

_____

d.

_____

Situation 4:

How can you handle this situation?

a.

_____

b.

_____

c.

_____

d.

_____

Homework

Client Homework

✎ Continue self-recording. Remember to use the back of your self-recording cards to write down the ways you handled your high-risk situations for the week.

✎ Complete the Warning Signs Worksheet.

Partner Homework

✎ Continue recording your partner's alcohol use, urges (intensity), and your level of relationship satisfaction.

✎ Complete the Warning Signs Worksheet.

Couple Homework

✎ Review the information in this chapter.

✎ Complete one problem-solving exercise at home. An additional copy of the Problem-Solving Worksheet can be found in the appendix.

✎ Hold at least one family meeting, using the steps reviewed in session.

✎ Complete the Warning Signs Worksheet.

Chapter 11

Session 11: Relapse Prevention Part III /
Acceptance Framework

Goals

- To learn about slips and relapses

- To learn ways of handling slips and relapses and to work with your partner to come up with a plan for handling slips and relapses

- To learn how to accept aspects of each other that may not change

Graphing Progress

As you have done every week, be sure to update your Alcohol Use and Urges and Relationship Satisfaction graphs in Chapter 2 using the information from your most recently completed self-recording cards.

Slips and Relapses

Slips can be very challenging. Even using your best skills you may still have difficulties. It will be easier for you in the long run if you don't, but it is possible that you will eventually take a drink, despite your best efforts. Sometimes people who slip give up on their abstinence goals and head back to drinking. If drinking occurs, it is important to realize that one drink does not have to inevitably lead to a full-blown relapse.

A person who slips can think of it in three ways:

1. The slip is a mistake that shouldn't be repeated. This is considered a lapse if the person does not continue drinking.

2. The slip is an opportunity to learn about something risky. The person should think of different ways to handle the situation in the future. This is considered a "prolapse" if the person does not continue drinking, but learns a lesson for the future.

3. The slip is a disaster, which shows that the person is hopeless. People who see the slip in this way think, "I have blown it. I will never succeed. I will just give up." Giving up and returning to drinking is called a relapse.

The third way of thinking is the worst choice. Slips are like falling off a bicycle. The fall may hurt, but you should get back on the bicycle and keep riding. You may feel rotten about the slip, but you can get back to remaining abstinent. The slip may even be an opportunity to learn about a difficult situation.

Handling Slips and Relapses

Looking for and thinking about warning signs help to prevent a slip. However, even people who work hard to remain abstinent may find themselves in an overwhelming situation. While you should work hard and expect to not take another drink, we believe you should be prepared for the possibility of a slip.

If you should take a drink, you have choices. As discussed previously, there are three different ways to think about the drink. You could think of it as a mistake (a slip), a mistake from which you learn something (a prolapse), or as a hopeless disaster (a relapse). The goal is never to have a relapse.

A drink does not have to become a relapse. If you ever have a drink, you should try to make it turn out to be a slip or prolapse. If you have a drink, remember the following:

1. **Don't panic.** One drink does not have to lead to an extended binge or a return to uncontrolled drinking.

2. **Stop, look, and listen.** Stop the ongoing flow of events and look and listen to what is happening. The lapse should be seen as a warning signal that you are in trouble. The lapse is like a flat tire—it is time to pull off the road to deal with the situation.

3. **Be aware of the abstinence violation effect.** Once you have a drink you may have thoughts such as, "I blew it," or "All our efforts were a waste," or "As long as I've blown it, I might as well keep drinking," or "My willpower has failed, I have no control," or "I'm addicted, and once I drink my body will take over." These thoughts might be accompanied by feelings of anger or guilt. It is crucial to dispute these thoughts immediately.

4. **Renew your commitment.** After a lapse, it is easy to feel discouraged and to want to give up. Think back over the reasons why you decided to change your drinking in the first place; look at your Decisional Matrix and think about all the positive long-term benefits of abstinence and the long-term problems associated with continued drinking.

5. **Decide on a course of action.** At a minimum, this should include:

    - Getting out of the drinking situation.
    - Waiting at least 2 hours before having a second drink.
    - Engaging in some activity during those 2 hours that would help avoid continued drinking. The activity might be a pleasurable one, or reviewing materials from treatment, or talking over the lapse with someone who could be helpful, or calling your therapist.

6. **Review the situation leading up to the lapse.** Don't blame yourself for what happened. By focusing on your own failings, you will feel guiltier and blame yourself more. Ask yourself, what events led up to the slip? What were the main triggers? Were there any early warning signs? Did you try to deal with these constructively? If not, why? Was your motivation weakened by fatigue, social pressure, depression? Once you have analyzed the slip, think about what changes you need to make to avoid future slips.

7. **Ask for help.** Make it easier on yourself by asking someone to help you either by encouraging you, giving you advice, distracting you, or engaging in some alternative activity with you. If you had a flat tire and your spare tire also was flat, you'd have to get help—a slip is the same situation.

Using the worksheet provided on the next page, write down some ideas for handling slips or relapses should they occur.

Plan for Handling Slips and Relapses

Immediate plans to prevent the slip from becoming a relapse:

_____

_____

_____

_____

How I will get support to handle the relapse?

_____

_____

_____

_____

The next day . . .

_____

_____

_____

_____

If drinking occurs, it is important that you know how to deal with it together. If you approach a slip the way you've learned to approach other problems, it will help you both get back on track more quickly. Open communication, use of X, Y, Z feedback, and good problem solving all can help.

Consider the following issues and come up with a couple's plan for handling slips and relapses.

1. What you should do or say to your partner if you drink, and how your partner could respond;

2. How your partner could initiate the conversation if he or she realizes that you have had something to drink, and how you could respond;

3. What steps you can take as a couple to respond to drinking; and

4. What, if any, limits your partner might place in terms of his or her response to drinking.

Discuss each of these issues, coming up with as specific a plan as possible for what to say or do. Write your plan on the worksheet on page 150.

Couple's Plan for Handling Slips or Relapses

1. Drinker: If I drink, I can say:

_____

_____

It would help if my partner said:

_____

_____

2. Partner: If I realize my partner drank, I can say:

_____

_____

It would help if he/she said:

_____

_____

3. Couple: If we both know a slip or relapse has occurred, we can:

_____

_____

4. [Optional] Partner: If my partner drank again, I would:

_____

_____

You have spent many weeks talking about change. The behaviors we wish to change are those that lead to drinking and problems in the relationship. Despite the focus on change, it is important to understand that people have limits to how much they can change. People are package deals—they have good and not-so-good qualities.

Most couples go through periods in which the partners do not see eye-to-eye. Every couple has to work out differences. One way is for the partners to change how they act toward one another. Another approach is to accept differences between you and your partner as something natural.

You can build greater happiness in your relationship by developing acceptance and/or tolerance. Acceptance happens when we develop a deeper understanding and appreciation for the pain of our partner. Through acceptance, we develop an understanding of our partner and learn the limits of how much change we can expect. Tolerance happens when we realize that our partner's irritating behavior will not change, but we learn how to live with it. Through building tolerance, we focus on our own reactions to the annoying behavior.

People who love each other can also hurt each other. The person who does something hurtful may not realize it. He or she may be feeling hurt as well. Strong, basic emotions tell us something important. Raw emotions—like anger or sadness—signal the violation of someone's basic values. When you see or feel these raw emotions, look for a basic issue that is important to you or your partner.

Differences between partners lead to unhealthy interactions. Three types of interactions signal problems created by different values:

The Mutual Trap happens when two people try to get out of a cycle of conflict, but nothing they do helps them break free. A common thought in this situation is "no matter what I do, he or she gets upset." Different approaches to thinking and handling problems create this trap. For example, one person may believe the best way to handle disagreements is not to show emotions. The other person may believe that the best way is to be open with emotions. These two people can get into a cycle of conflict because their beliefs are so different. One person wants to talk about emotions; the other wants to avoid expressing feelings. These two people may feel that they're in a no-win situation.

The Minefield refers to special topics that trigger bigger conflicts. Everybody is sensitive about some topic or other. Certain topics "push a button" that leads to arguments. For example, one person may get upset if his or her partner complains about how money is spent. The person who gets upset may not just react to the one complaint, but to something else behind the complaint. The complaint may sound like an old criticism or disagreement that was never settled.

The Credibility Gap happens when one person will not believe that the other person is trying to "make-up" after a conflict. Anger or hurt feelings will affect how someone interprets what another person is doing. These feelings can block a person from seeing honest attempts to make up.

How do you get past the unhealthy cycles? Two people look and react to a situation in different ways. The first step to building tolerance for some things your partner does is to understand some of these differences. Ask yourself several questions:

- How do I contribute to the problem?

- What changes can I make to improve the situation?

- What can I do to make me feel better about the situation? What can I do for myself?

- How does my partner see the problem?

- How do my actions affect my partner?

- What are the things that I like about my partner?

- What are the good things about my partner's behavior? If seen a different way, would someone consider the behavior as a good quality?

- Can I realistically expect him or her to change to be exactly what I want?

Often the irritating behaviors of our partners can also be good qualities. Stubbornness can also be patience. Stuffiness can also be discipline. Flightiness can also be free-spiritedness. A quality you once found attractive in your partner can later become something irritating. For example, someone who is fun and free-spirited may become irritating because he or she cannot plan well.

Strategies for Building Acceptance

1. Develop a better understanding about how your partner feels in the situation. Find the soft emotions behind the angry words. Often during arguments, partners only show hard emotions: anger, contempt, or disgust.

The hard emotions come out as accusations. An angry person may think his or her partner is a "bad" person. He or she may accuse the other person of being mean, selfish, inconsiderate, hysterical, moody, and so on. These big labels interfere with creating a healthy relationship. Underneath the hard emotions are soft emotions: sadness, fear, or hurt. These emotions reflect the personal pain that someone is suffering. Hurt can come from feeling insulted, unappreciated, or overpowered by the other person. Unhealthy conflict is a mixture of both soft and hard emotions.

The key to changing this cycle is to remove the accusations from the pain. Seeing and understanding each other's pain will help you develop a greater appreciation for the other person. Showing pain to your partner allows the other person an opportunity to understand your position better. Instead of focusing on what is wrong with your partner, focus on how you feel about the situation. Show him or her the soft rather than the hard emotions. Exposing soft emotions to your partner will allow him or her to see the impact of his or her actions. Also, by focusing on the soft emotions, you begin to help yourself rather than trying to change your partner.

2. Another approach to handling a conflict is to think of the problem as the enemy outside the relationship. Think of the problem as an "it" and not as something terribly wrong with your partner. The problem will become clearer if you see "it" as something impersonal rather than a defect in your partner. Learn to accept that certain topics are "hot spots" that the two of you have to face together.

If you can't accept something, you can learn tolerance. Even if your partner's behavior is too hard to accept, you can change how much it affects you. Tolerance happens when we realize that our partner's behavior will not change completely and we develop a better way to handle our own reactions. Something he or she does may irritate or enrage you. Part of your reaction comes from how you see the behavior. One way to change this is to look at the behavior differently. Ask yourself several questions: why does it affect you so much? If someone else did the same thing, would I be so upset?

Often, an irritating behavior will have its benefits. For example, someone may become annoyed with his or her partner's slow and methodical attention to the details of a job. This behavior may be useful for boring and complicated chores. Another example is that of someone who may get angry because his or her partner never shows up on time. This behavior may be part of a free-spiritedness that is attractive. Many annoying behaviors have their attractive sides.

High-Risk Situations for the Week

Work with your therapist and partner to identify at least one high-risk situation coming up in the next week. Write down ideas about how to handle this situation on the High-Risk Situations worksheet. Use the back of your self-recording card to record how you actually handled the anticipated situation, and write down any unexpected high-risk situations that may have arisen during the week.

High-Risk Situations

What high-risk situations do you think you may experience this week?

Situation 1:

How can you handle this situation?

a.

b.

c.

d.

Situation 2:

How can you handle this situation?

a.

b.

c.

d.

Situation 3:

How can you handle this situation?

a.

b.

c.

d.

Situation 4:

How can you handle this situation?

a.

b.

c.

d.

Homework

Client Homework

✎ Continue self-recording. Remember to use the back of your self-recording cards to write down the ways you handled your high-risk situations for the week.

✎ Think about one characteristic of your partner that you will focus on learning to accept.

Partner Homework

✎ Continue recording your partner's alcohol use, urges (intensity), and your level of relationship satisfaction.

✎ Think about one characteristic of your partner that you will focus on learning to accept.

Couple Homework

✎ Review the information in this chapter.

✎ Finish your couple's plan for handling slips and relapses and role-play one scenario at home if not done in session.

Chapter 12

Session 12: Review / Relapse Prevention Part IV

Goals

- To identify the skills you will continue to use to maintain your progress in the future

- To create and sign a relapse contract

Graphing Progress

As you have done every week, be sure to update your Alcohol Use and Urges and Relationship Satisfaction graphs in Chapter 2 using the information from your most recently completed self-recording cards. You should see a marked improvement in your level of relationship satisfaction and a decrease in your urges to drink alcohol, compared to when you first started this program. Take some time to look at the graphs and think about all that you've done to create these changes.

The End of Treatment

This week marks the end of the program and your final session with your therapist. The goal of this session is to remind you that you now have the skills to remain abstinent, that your partner has better ways to cope with drinking-related issues, and that you both are well on your way to a happier and healthier relationship. You have learned a set of skills that can be applied in everyday life to deal with high-risk situations. The relapse-prevention techniques you have been taught will help you maintain gains made during treatment. Control of your life is now back in your own hands.

Client Skills

Think about the skills you have learned in this program (e.g., self-recording, identifying positive alternatives to drinking, relapse-prevention strategies) and identify the ones that have been most important to the changes you have made. Which skills will you continue to use in order to maintain progress now that treatment is ending? Write them down in the space provided.

1 _____

2 _____

3 _____

Partner Skills

Think about the skills you have learned in this program that have helped you to cope with your partner's drinking (e.g., providing support, decreasing triggers for drinking, not protecting your partner from the negative consequences of drinking). Identify the skills that have been most important and write them down in the space provided.

1 _____

2 _____

3 _____

Couple Skills

Together, think about the skills you have learned in this program that have helped you to build a better relationship (e.g., sharing activities, good communication, "notice something nice"). Identify the most important changes you have made and write them down in the space provided.

1 _____

2 _____

3 _____

Relapse Contract

Think about the things you are willing to do in order to prevent relapse. Write down your thoughts in the space provided and use them to create a relapse contract that you, your partner, and your therapist can sign. A sample relapse contract is also provided to give you an idea of how to format your own contract.

Client—What I will do to prevent relapse:

_____

_____

_____

_____

Partner—What I will do to help my partner avoid relapse:

_____

_____

_____

_____

Sample Relapse Contract

1. If I drink alcohol at all, in any amount, I will sit down the following day and review what to do in the event of a relapse. I will use my trigger sheets to figure out what happened. I will tell my partner and ask for his or her support.

2. If I drink again within a month, I will call my therapist with the goal of getting a referral to get back into treatment.

3. If I drink even once in a binge (out of control) fashion, I will call, with the goal of getting back into treatment.

4. My goal is to remain abstinent for at least _____. At that time I will re-evaluate this contract and write a new one.

_____   _____

Client Signature   Date

1. If _____ drinks, I will ask how I can help him or her. I will not yell.

2. If he or she keeps drinking, I will suggest that we call to get more treatment.

3. If he or she refuses help and keeps drinking, I will call for help for myself.

_____   _____

Partner Signature   Date

_____   _____

Therapist Signature   Date

Congratulations on successfully completing this program! You have worked very hard and we hope that you have seen improvement in not only the drinking problem but also in your relationship with one another. Remember the keys to maintaining your success: (1) keep motivated by remembering the problems that drinking created and the good that has come from not drinking; (2) use the skills you've learned; (3) accept that change is difficult—not every day will be easy—and that the most successful people learn how to ride out the tough times; (4) rely on each other when you can; (5) find ways to enjoy your lives and each other each day; (6) know that there always is help available if you need it—don't be embarrassed to ask.

Appendix of Forms

Behavior Chain

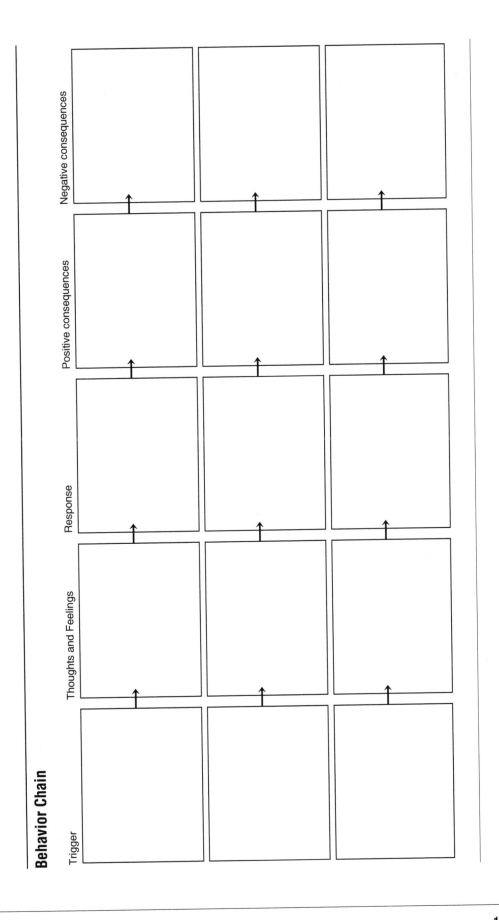

Trigger → Thoughts and Feelings → Response → Positive consequences → Negative consequences

Self-Management Planning Sheet

Trigger	Plan	+\−Consequences	Difficulty (1–10)
I.			
2.			

Partner Self-Management Planning Sheet

Trigger	Plan	+/−Consequences	Difficulty (1–10)
1.			
2.			

Problem-Solving Worksheet

Pick a problem that has come up in the course of treatment so far and practice solving it using the methods just described.

1. Gather Information: _____

2. Problem Definition: _____

3. Brainstorming for Solutions and Listing of Pros and Cons:

Solution	Pros (short and long term)	Cons (short and long term)
a.		
b.		
c.		
d.		
e.		

4. Pick solution(s): _____

5. Implement the solution for a period of time.

6. Reevaluate the solution—Did it work? _____

If not, do problem solving again.

Client Self-Monitoring Cards

Client Self-Monitoring Card

Date _____

Daily monitoring

Urges

Time	How strong? (1–7)	Trigger		

Drinks

Time	Type of drink	Amount (in ounces)	% Alcohol	Trigger

Relationship Satisfaction   1   2   3   4   5   6   7

                         very low   greatest ever

For woman only   Do you have your menstrual period today?   Yes   No   N/A

Client Self-Monitoring Card

Daily monitoring

Date _____

Urges

Time	How strong? (1–7)	Trigger			

Drinks

Time	Type of drink	Amount (in ounces)	% Alcohol	Trigger

Relationship Satisfaction   1   2   3   4   5   6   7
                               very low   greatest ever

For woman only   Do you have your menstrual period today?   Yes   No   N/A

Client Self-Monitoring Card

Date _____

Daily monitoring

Urges

Time	How strong? (1–7)	Trigger

Drinks

Time	Type of drink	Amount (in ounces)	% Alcohol	Trigger

Relationship Satisfaction

1	2	3	4	5	6	7
very low						greatest ever

For woman only   Do you have your menstrual period today?   Yes   No   N/A

Client Self-Monitoring Card

Date _____

Daily monitoring

Urges

Time	How strong? (1–7)	Trigger

Drinks

Time	Type of drink	Amount (in ounces)	% Alcohol	Trigger

Relationship Satisfaction

1	2	3	4	5	6	7
very low						greatest ever

For woman only   Do you have your menstrual period today?   Yes   No   N/A

Client Self-Monitoring Card

Date _____

Daily monitoring

Urges

Time	How strong? (1–7)	Trigger

Drinks

Time	Type of drink	Amount (in ounces)	% Alcohol	Trigger

Relationship Satisfaction
1   2   3   4   5   6   7
very low   greatest ever

For woman only   Do you have your menstrual period today?   Yes   No   N/A

Client Self-Monitoring Card

Date _____

Daily monitoring

Urges

Time	How strong? (1–7)	Trigger

Drinks

Time	Type of drink	Amount (in ounces)	% Alcohol	Trigger

Relationship Satisfaction   1   2   3   4   5   6   7

                    very low   greatest ever

For woman only   Do you have your menstrual period today?   Yes   No   N/A

Client Self-Monitoring Card

Date _____

Daily monitoring

Urges

Time	How strong? (1–7)	Trigger

Drinks

Time	Type of drink	Amount (in ounces)	% Alcohol	Trigger

Relationship Satisfaction   1   2   3   4   5   6   7

very low   greatest ever

For woman only   Do you have your menstrual period today?   Yes   No   N/A

Client Self-Monitoring Card

Date _____

Daily monitoring

Urges

Time	How strong? (1–7)	Trigger

Drinks

Time	Type of drink	Amount (in ounces)	% Alcohol	Trigger

Relationship Satisfaction	1	2	3	4	5	6	7
	very low						greatest ever

For woman only   Do you have your menstrual period today?   Yes   No   N/A

Client Self-Monitoring Card

Date _____

Daily monitoring

Urges

Time	How strong? (1–7)	Trigger				

Drinks

Time	Type of drink	Amount (in ounces)	% Alcohol	Trigger

Relationship Satisfaction

1	2	3	4	5	6	7
very low						greatest ever

For woman only — Do you have your menstrual period today?   Yes   No   N/A

Client Self-Monitoring Card

Date _____

Daily monitoring

Urges

Time	How strong? (1–7)	Trigger

Drinks

Time	Type of drink	Amount (in ounces)	% Alcohol	Trigger

Relationship Satisfaction   1   2   3   4   5   6   7

                             very low   greatest ever

For woman only   Do you have your menstrual period today?   Yes   No   N/A

Client Self-Monitoring Card

Date _____

Daily monitoring

Urges

Time	How strong? (1–7)	Trigger

Drinks

Time	Type of drink	Amount (in ounces)	% Alcohol	Trigger

Relationship Satisfaction

1	2	3	4	5	6	7
very low						greatest ever

For woman only   Do you have your menstrual period today?   Yes   No   N/A

Client Self-Monitoring Card

Date _____

Daily monitoring

Urges

Time	How strong? (1–7)	Trigger

Drinks

Time	Type of drink	Amount (in ounces)	% Alcohol	Trigger

Relationship Satisfaction

1	2	3	4	5	6	7
very low						greatest ever

For woman only — Do you have your menstrual period today?   Yes   No   N/A

Client Self-Monitoring Card

Date _____

Daily monitoring

Urges

Time	How strong? (1–7)	Trigger

Drinks

Time	Type of drink	Amount (in ounces)	% Alcohol	Trigger

Relationship Satisfaction

1	2	3	4	5	6	7
very low						greatest ever

For woman only   Do you have your menstrual period today?   Yes   No   N/A

Client Self-Monitoring Card

Date _____

Daily monitoring

Urges

Time	How strong? (1–7)	Trigger			Drinks				
					Time	**Type of drink**	**Amount (in ounces)**	**% Alcohol**	**Trigger**

Relationship Satisfaction	1 very low	2	3	4	5	6	7 greatest ever

For woman only   Do you have your menstrual period today?   Yes   No   N/A

Partner Recording Cards

Partner Recording Card

Partner monitoring

Day	Date	Drinking	Drug use	Urge intensity	Relationship satisfaction
		NO L M H	Y N	0 1 2 3 4 5 6 7	1 2 3 4 5 6 7
		NO L M H	Y N	0 1 2 3 4 5 6 7	1 2 3 4 5 6 7
		NO L M H	Y N	0 1 2 3 4 5 6 7	1 2 3 4 5 6 7
		NO L M H	Y N	0 1 2 3 4 5 6 7	1 2 3 4 5 6 7
		NO L M H	Y N	0 1 2 3 4 5 6 7	1 2 3 4 5 6 7
		NO L M H	Y N	0 1 2 3 4 5 6 7	1 2 3 4 5 6 7
		NO L M H	Y N	0 1 2 3 4 5 6 7	1 2 3 4 5 6 7

Partner Recording Card

Partner monitoring

Day	Date	Drinking	Drug use	Urge intensity	Relationship satisfaction
		NO L M H	Y N	0 1 2 3 4 5 6 7	1 2 3 4 5 6 7
		NO L M H	Y N	0 1 2 3 4 5 6 7	1 2 3 4 5 6 7
		NO L M H	Y N	0 1 2 3 4 5 6 7	1 2 3 4 5 6 7
		NO L M H	Y N	0 1 2 3 4 5 6 7	1 2 3 4 5 6 7
		NO L M H	Y N	0 1 2 3 4 5 6 7	1 2 3 4 5 6 7
		NO L M H	Y N	0 1 2 3 4 5 6 7	1 2 3 4 5 6 7
		NO L M H	Y N	0 1 2 3 4 5 6 7	1 2 3 4 5 6 7

Partner Recording Card

Partner monitoring

Day	Date	Drinking	Drug use	Urge intensity	Relationship satisfaction
		NO L M H	Y N	0 1 2 3 4 5 6 7	1 2 3 4 5 6 7
		NO L M H	Y N	0 1 2 3 4 5 6 7	1 2 3 4 5 6 7
		NO L M H	Y N	0 1 2 3 4 5 6 7	1 2 3 4 5 6 7
		NO L M H	Y N	0 1 2 3 4 5 6 7	1 2 3 4 5 6 7
		NO L M H	Y N	0 1 2 3 4 5 6 7	1 2 3 4 5 6 7
		NO L M H	Y N	0 1 2 3 4 5 6 7	1 2 3 4 5 6 7
		NO L M H	Y N	0 1 2 3 4 5 6 7	1 2 3 4 5 6 7

Partner Recording Card

Partner monitoring

Day	Date	Drinking	Drug use	Urge intensity	Relationship satisfaction
		NO L M H	Y N	0 1 2 3 4 5 6 7	1 2 3 4 5 6 7
		NO L M H	Y N	0 1 2 3 4 5 6 7	1 2 3 4 5 6 7
		NO L M H	Y N	0 1 2 3 4 5 6 7	1 2 3 4 5 6 7
		NO L M H	Y N	0 1 2 3 4 5 6 7	1 2 3 4 5 6 7
		NO L M H	Y N	0 1 2 3 4 5 6 7	1 2 3 4 5 6 7
		NO L M H	Y N	0 1 2 3 4 5 6 7	1 2 3 4 5 6 7
		NO L M H	Y N	0 1 2 3 4 5 6 7	1 2 3 4 5 6 7

Partner Recording Card

Partner monitoring

Day	Date	Drinking	Drug use	Urge intensity	Relationship satisfaction
		NO L M H	Y N	0 1 2 3 4 5 6 7	1 2 3 4 5 6 7
		NO L M H	Y N	0 1 2 3 4 5 6 7	1 2 3 4 5 6 7
		NO L M H	Y N	0 1 2 3 4 5 6 7	1 2 3 4 5 6 7
		NO L M H	Y N	0 1 2 3 4 5 6 7	1 2 3 4 5 6 7
		NO L M H	Y N	0 1 2 3 4 5 6 7	1 2 3 4 5 6 7
		NO L M H	Y N	0 1 2 3 4 5 6 7	1 2 3 4 5 6 7
		NO L M H	Y N	0 1 2 3 4 5 6 7	1 2 3 4 5 6 7

Partner Recording Card

Partner monitoring

Day	Date	Drinking	Drug use	Urge intensity	Relationship satisfaction
		NO L M H	Y N	0 1 2 3 4 5 6 7	1 2 3 4 5 6 7
		NO L M H	Y N	0 1 2 3 4 5 6 7	1 2 3 4 5 6 7
		NO L M H	Y N	0 1 2 3 4 5 6 7	1 2 3 4 5 6 7
		NO L M H	Y N	0 1 2 3 4 5 6 7	1 2 3 4 5 6 7
		NO L M H	Y N	0 1 2 3 4 5 6 7	1 2 3 4 5 6 7
		NO L M H	Y N	0 1 2 3 4 5 6 7	1 2 3 4 5 6 7
		NO L M H	Y N	0 1 2 3 4 5 6 7	1 2 3 4 5 6 7

Partner Recording Card

Partner monitoring

Day	Date	Drinking	Drug use	Urge intensity	Relationship satisfaction
		NO L M H	Y N	0 1 2 3 4 5 6 7	1 2 3 4 5 6 7
		NO L M H	Y N	0 1 2 3 4 5 6 7	1 2 3 4 5 6 7
		NO L M H	Y N	0 1 2 3 4 5 6 7	1 2 3 4 5 6 7
		NO L M H	Y N	0 1 2 3 4 5 6 7	1 2 3 4 5 6 7
		NO L M H	Y N	0 1 2 3 4 5 6 7	1 2 3 4 5 6 7
		NO L M H	Y N	0 1 2 3 4 5 6 7	1 2 3 4 5 6 7
		NO L M H	Y N	0 1 2 3 4 5 6 7	1 2 3 4 5 6 7

213

Partner Recording Card

Partner monitoring

Day	Date	Drinking	Drug use	Urge intensity	Relationship satisfaction
		NO L M H	Y N	0 1 2 3 4 5 6 7	1 2 3 4 5 6 7
		NO L M H	Y N	0 1 2 3 4 5 6 7	1 2 3 4 5 6 7
		NO L M H	Y N	0 1 2 3 4 5 6 7	1 2 3 4 5 6 7
		NO L M H	Y N	0 1 2 3 4 5 6 7	1 2 3 4 5 6 7
		NO L M H	Y N	0 1 2 3 4 5 6 7	1 2 3 4 5 6 7
		NO L M H	Y N	0 1 2 3 4 5 6 7	1 2 3 4 5 6 7
		NO L M H	Y N	0 1 2 3 4 5 6 7	1 2 3 4 5 6 7

Partner Recording Card

Partner monitoring

Day	Date	Drinking	Drug use	Urge intensity	Relationship satisfaction
		NO L M H	Y N	0 1 2 3 4 5 6 7	1 2 3 4 5 6 7
		NO L M H	Y N	0 1 2 3 4 5 6 7	1 2 3 4 5 6 7
		NO L M H	Y N	0 1 2 3 4 5 6 7	1 2 3 4 5 6 7
		NO L M H	Y N	0 1 2 3 4 5 6 7	1 2 3 4 5 6 7
		NO L M H	Y N	0 1 2 3 4 5 6 7	1 2 3 4 5 6 7
		NO L M H	Y N	0 1 2 3 4 5 6 7	1 2 3 4 5 6 7
		NO L M H	Y N	0 1 2 3 4 5 6 7	1 2 3 4 5 6 7

Partner Recording Card

Partner monitoring

Day	Date	Drinking	Drug use	Urge intensity	Relationship satisfaction
		NO L M H	Y N	0 1 2 3 4 5 6 7	1 2 3 4 5 6 7
		NO L M H	Y N	0 1 2 3 4 5 6 7	1 2 3 4 5 6 7
		NO L M H	Y N	0 1 2 3 4 5 6 7	1 2 3 4 5 6 7
		NO L M H	Y N	0 1 2 3 4 5 6 7	1 2 3 4 5 6 7
		NO L M H	Y N	0 1 2 3 4 5 6 7	1 2 3 4 5 6 7
		NO L M H	Y N	0 1 2 3 4 5 6 7	1 2 3 4 5 6 7
		NO L M H	Y N	0 1 2 3 4 5 6 7	1 2 3 4 5 6 7

Partner Recording Card

Partner monitoring

Day	Date	Drinking	Drug use	Urge intensity	Relationship satisfaction
		NO L M H	Y N	0 1 2 3 4 5 6 7	1 2 3 4 5 6 7
		NO L M H	Y N	0 1 2 3 4 5 6 7	1 2 3 4 5 6 7
		NO L M H	Y N	0 1 2 3 4 5 6 7	1 2 3 4 5 6 7
		NO L M H	Y N	0 1 2 3 4 5 6 7	1 2 3 4 5 6 7
		NO L M H	Y N	0 1 2 3 4 5 6 7	1 2 3 4 5 6 7
		NO L M H	Y N	0 1 2 3 4 5 6 7	1 2 3 4 5 6 7
		NO L M H	Y N	0 1 2 3 4 5 6 7	1 2 3 4 5 6 7

Partner Recording Card

Partner monitoring

Day	Date	Drinking	Drug use	Urge intensity	Relationship satisfaction
		NO L M H	Y N	0 1 2 3 4 5 6 7	1 2 3 4 5 6 7
		NO L M H	Y N	0 1 2 3 4 5 6 7	1 2 3 4 5 6 7
		NO L M H	Y N	0 1 2 3 4 5 6 7	1 2 3 4 5 6 7
		NO L M H	Y N	0 1 2 3 4 5 6 7	1 2 3 4 5 6 7
		NO L M H	Y N	0 1 2 3 4 5 6 7	1 2 3 4 5 6 7
		NO L M H	Y N	0 1 2 3 4 5 6 7	1 2 3 4 5 6 7
		NO L M H	Y N	0 1 2 3 4 5 6 7	1 2 3 4 5 6 7

Lightning Source UK Ltd.
Milton Keynes UK
UKHW030939060121
376493UK00005B/76